Sketches from
Behind Prison Walls

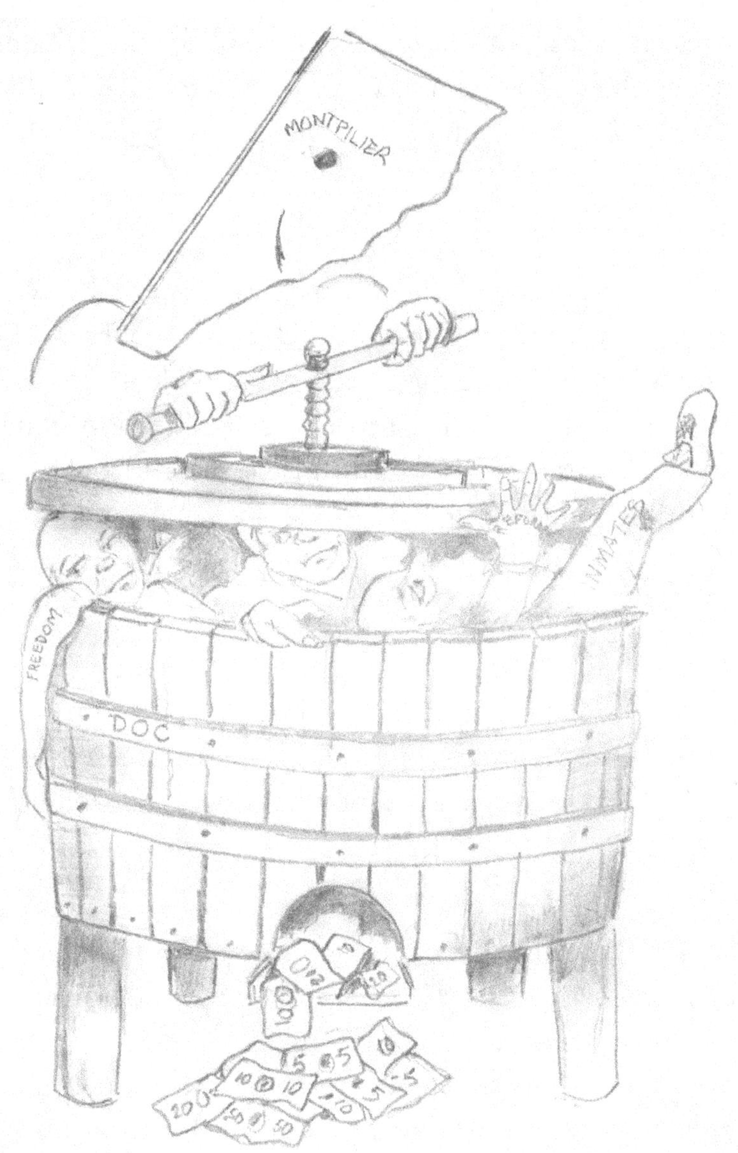

Praise for *Sketches from Behind Prison Walls*

Rein Kolts and Devon Kurtz have created a powerful book. It does not have the retributive power of the system that has placed Kolts and his compatriots in prison, but the power of the artist, the power to confer empathy. Kolts' sktches of those enchained—and his records of their testimonies—call forth their subjects and link us with them, as witnesses and fellow men. Kurtz, as interlocutor and advocate, has thoughtfully presented the lives of these men whom many of us in convenience, in guilt, choose to forget. —Mickal Adler, art writer & curator

The journey of personal growth is expressed in many ways. We each have inspiration inside of us and for some the expression of this journey is harder than others. *Sketches from Behind Prison Walls* allows us all to join in the growth journeys of individuals learning through adversity and gives us a window of empathy to those going through self-reflection, rehabilitation, and recovery. This inspirational depiction of art taps into the promise of tomorrow for these incarcerated individuals and the communities they will join upon their release.

—Dr. Armin McCrea-Dastur, organizational culture expert

Sketches from Behind Prison Walls is not just an artistic endeavor; it is a plea for justice, a call for empathy, and a testament to the resilience of the human spirit. It reminds us that, even in the darkest of circumstances, beauty can flourish, voices can unite to break through silence, and every person, no matter their situation, has an intrinsic value that deserves recognition and respect.

—Brian Koehn, social entrepreneur and former prison warden

Sketches from Behind Prison Walls offers an unflinching and empathetic glimpse into the lives of the incarcerated, blending art and narrative to humanize and challenge our perceptions of justice. It serves as a potent call to action for reform, urging readers to recognize the dignity and humanity within prison walls. A must-read for anyone committed to understanding and transforming our criminal justice system.   —Adam Clausen, prison reform advocate and formerly incarcerated

Quaker Institute for the Future

The Quaker Institute for the Future (QIF) is pleased to publish this book, a collaborative effort among men incarcerated in a Vermont prison, artist Rein Kolts, and writer Devon Kurtz.

QIF is a community of scholars, artists, and authors whose work grows from our commitment to honoring the Divine in all of Life by growing our writing and art out of the Spirit. Historically, QIF thinkers have analyzed Earth systems, with humans among the forces at work. QIF artists have made individual lives visible within those systems, in their joys and their agonies.

Sketches from Behind Prison Walls falls within this tradition. The face of the system that has imprisoned these men appears most clearly in the picture of Justice in Vermont, where money outweighs lives and the lives have no defenders in the official machinery. Those outweighed could as easily be forests or rivers or the victims of wars, as predictably as the men in this Vermont prison. Punishment is a manifestation of power-over. Making prison a healing process would be a manifestation of power-with.

Mass incarceration in the United States, which imprisons by far the largest share of its population of any country, is the domestic partner of its vast global military presence. The two institutions are joined technologically and culturally. The men whose words and faces appear in this book are actors in a world drama, with scenes being enacted thousands of miles away from them as well as nearby.

Devon Kurtz received modest financial support from QIF for his part in this collaboration. We are honored by our small role in the result.

Susan Cozzens, Alternate Clerk
Quaker Institute for the Future

To my Uncle Kenny:
who devoted his life to serving God and the souls of those on the fringe.

Sketches from Behind Prison Walls

Illustrated by Rein Kolts

Introduction and Commentary by Devon M. Kurtz

Published for Quaker Institute for the Future by Producciones de la Hamaca, Caye Caulker, Belize.
<producciones-hamaca.com>

ISBN: 978-976-43-7   (paperback edition)
ISBN: 978-976-44-4   (e-book edition)
ISBN: 978-976-45-1   (hard-back edition)

This book was printed on-demand by Lightning Source, Inc (LSI). The on-demand printing system is environmentally friendly because books are printed as needed, instead of in large numbers that might end up in someone's basement or a dump site. I addition, LSI is committed to using materials obtained by sustainable forestry practices. LSI is certified by Sustainable Forestry Initiative (SFI® Certificate Number: PwC-SFICOC-345 SFI-00980). The Sustainable Forestry Initiative is an independent, internationally recognized non-profit organization responsible for the SFI certification standard, the world's largest single forest certification standard. The SFI program is based on the premise that responsible environmental behavior and sound business decisions can co-exist to the benefit of communities, customers and the environment, today and for future generations <sfiprogram.org>.

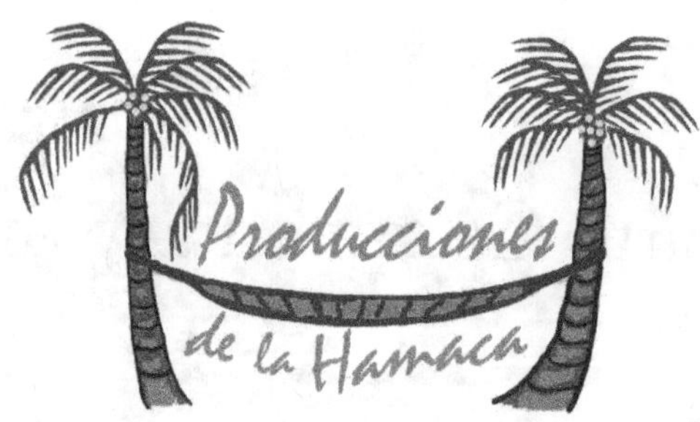

Producciones de la Hamaca is dedicated to:
—Celebration and documentation of Earth and all her inhabitants,
—Restoration and conservation of Earth's natural resources,
—Creative expression of the sacredness of Earth and Spirit.

Table of Contents

Preface

I met Rein Kolts in a shabby cinder block visiting room washed out in fluorescent lighting. He was bigger than many of the other guys—and older. But he lumbered into the room with an effervescent smile that contrasted with the environment: prison. He was shocked and full of delight to see me: "A Quaker! The cavalry's here at last!"

Rein, a lifelong Quaker who tended to wounded soldiers as compensatory service when he was a conscientious objector during the Vietnam War, knew how rare it is to encounter other Quakers. Truthfully, when I started a Quaker worship service at Southern State Correctional Facility in Springfield, Vermont, I did not expect to encounter a single Quaker either. With fewer than eighty thousand followers in America and without the kind of close knit religious communities of other faiths, Quakers are a scarce presence in American society.

Then I met Rein, one of the few Quakers actually in prison. At twenty-five years old and with no formal ministry training, I had set out alone into the daunting environment of America's sprawling system of mass incarceration. I had no idea what to expect, or how I might be received. When Rein greeted me, I felt relief settle over me—I had an ally in him at least.

Rein joined my worship group regularly over the months that followed. Despite being in prison, he embodied his Quaker values, living with a deep commitment to service and empowering others. Eventually, he shared with me his primary medium for helping others: his art.

Rein started sketching other inmates and asking them to write journal entries a few years before I met him. He saw it as a way to both bring them joy and convey to them that they matter. But as the collection steadily grew, it took on a greater purpose.

I was moved by the extraordinary intimacy and authenticity of Rein's work. He collected powerful accounts from his peers in prison and amplified their voices through his portraits of them. It was clear to me that this collection had enormous potential to confront the disinterest and disdain of the public towards incarcerated people. In large part, I felt this way because these stories and portraits dealt primarily with what one's life is like in prison, rather than how he got there. Much cultural attention is paid to satiating the public's morbid curiosities about "true crime" and questions of whether someone is innocent or guilty. Political conversations about prison point to macro-level trends like mass incarceration. In every aspect of public life, minimal attention is paid to the individual lives of people in prison, especially those who are guilty of serious crimes. What I love most about this collection is that it does not get mired in these more fashionable but less authentic aspects of the criminal justice system. As a result, this book fosters a more nuanced understanding of the people who populate America's prisons and expresses their inherent dignity and humanity beyond questions of innocence, guilt, or politics.

Rein and the other incarcerated men who contributed to this book have unique voices beyond the drone of conventional narratives of America's criminal justice system. We should listen to them, see them, and try to understand them. In doing so, we will grasp difficult truths about our society and its injustices; we will learn about ourselves and how we have contributed to creating a system that smothers the souls of those ensnared in it; and most of all, we will see the hope and endurance of people who have little reason to have either, and yet they overcome.

Acknowledgements

This book is a testament to the faith Rein Kolts put in me. I am grateful to Rein and his wife, Karin, for including me in the early version of this collection and trusting me with its development and care while Rein remained in prison.

I also thank Elijah Oaks, my dear friend and colleague, who never fails to answer my calls for strange requests, whether it involves taxidermy, occult rituals, or controversial literature. Eli was instrumental in compiling and revising the early manuscript and otherwise motivating me to continue the project.

This book, and further, my work in prison ministry, would not have been possible without the Quakers of Hanover Friends Meeting, and especially my spiritual anchors, Rhea McKay, Richard Morse, Fran Brokaw, and Lindsay Dearborn. After a lifetime of searching for a spiritual home, I was warmly welcomed by them.

I am grateful for the financial support of the Legacy Grant Committee of the New England Yearly Meeting, with which this project was funded. I also thank Gray Cox, Judy Lumb, and the Quaker Institute for the Future for their hard work in realizing my vision for this book.

Finally, I thank my uncle, Kenny Kurtz, who demonstrated to me a life of faithful humility and service in his career as a correctional officer in the U.S. Bureau of Prisons and a devoted Twelve Step mentor. He inspires me to continue the fight for better prisons, even if it will not be realized in my lifetime.

Devon M. Kurtz

Illustrator's Note

This book is a collaborative creation of the inmates of the Vermont Department of Corrections, born of the frustration and despair that accompanies our captivity. The stories and artwork herein are, for most of us, our only voice—whispers that collectively amplify into a shout for justice. No two of us followed the same pathway to prison, but from the unfortunate position at which our paths have crossed we have endeavored to create beauty in the face of the horrors of our reality.

My name is Rein Kolts. I am an artist imprisoned at the Southern State Correctional Facility in Springfield, Vermont. I began sketching my fellow inmates mostly as a way to pass my time productively and bring a modicum of joy to the other men and their families. Drawing a person fosters a certain intimacy and friendship with them, and I found that through my art I earned the vulnerability of the men I drew. Some inmates spoke of their children or a distant lover. Others raged against the courts or the prison administration. Many expressed exasperation, some found faith, but all hungered for purpose.

We started to write down our stories to accompany my sketches. What started as a pass-time transformed into collective expression that had the potential to overcome the loss of our voices at the hands of the criminal justice system. No one listens to one of us—but maybe they would hear us if we spoke together. Maybe they could see us if we were transformed into art and beauty.

Chains, cell blocks, and chemical sprays have a way of signifying to the people subjected to them that they do not matter—that they are meant to be dominated and incapacitated. To the public, seeing your government subject people to domination signifies that those people probably needed to be dominated to keep you safe. And we, the subjects of domination, lose our time, our voices, our dignity, our humanity, and too often, our lives. In just the last year, two percent of the inmates at Southern State Correctional Facility have died.

We know how little we matter to the state. But through our art and our stories, I hope we can convince you that we should matter to you.

Rein Kolts

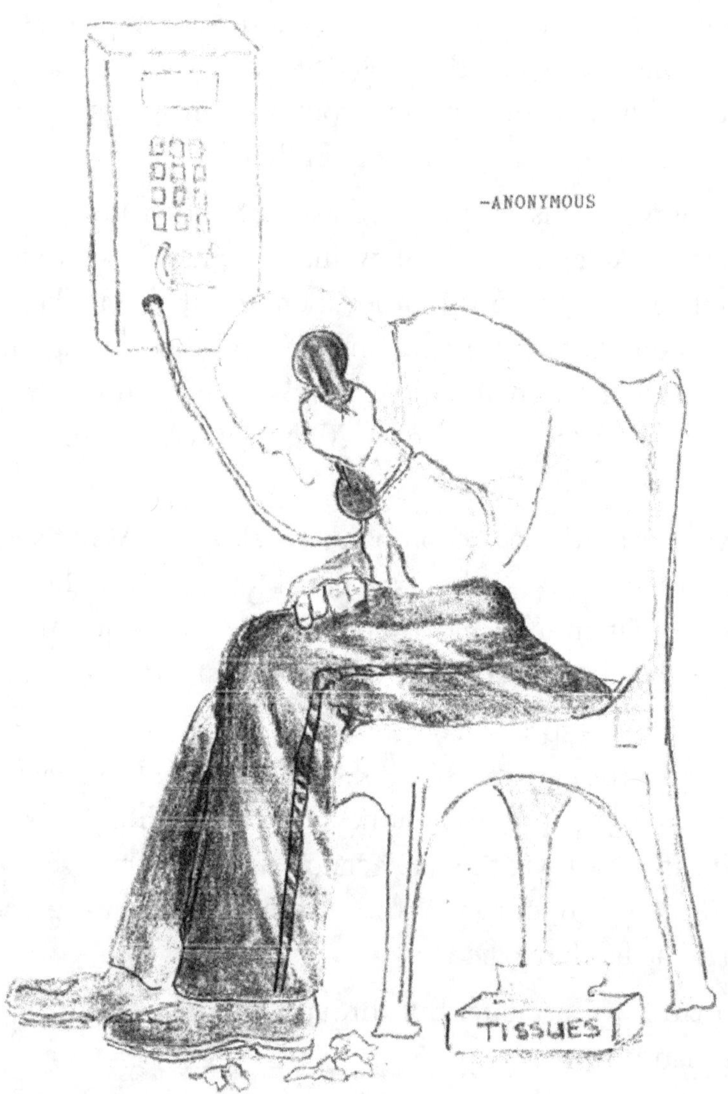

—ANONYMOUS

The Fate I Deserved?

I think of my sentence and the Time That I've served, a crime was committed
Was it the fate I deserved, a box full of strangers
The story was told, they passed down their verdict
My life's now on hold.
They don't know the whole story,
just what they've heard
But No, you can't speak, so don't say a word
A lawyer has been chosen, he'll speak up for you,
But that's not what happened, now what do I do?
You won't let me speak, the truth has been lost
But you got your conviction, no matter the cost.
But this is my case, and wouldn't you know it,
It's just one more rhyme from this jailhouse POET.
                    —a Jailhouse Poet
                        Southern State Correctional Facility

Introduction

America has a preoccupation with prison.

More than half a century ago, Johnny Cash's albums At San Quentin and At Folsom Prison anticipated the ways in which the aesthetics of prison would become a regrettable part of Americana. More than just their lyrical content, these albums use live recordings from within prisons to expose Americans to a facet of civilized society that most of us prefer not to encounter or imagine.

At the time of Johnny Cash's unusual decision to record two new albums in live concerts for inmates, America's prison population was barely 200,000—or 1 person for every 1,000 citizens. Today, America imprisons more than 1.2 million people, or more than 5 people per 1,000 citizens. By every metric, the prison system touches more Americans than ever.

This collection contains a series of sketched portraits by artist Rein Kolts, an inmate at Southern State Correctional Facility, accompanied by personal literature from the incarcerated men whom he depicts. Together, these pairings are an uncomfortably honest interpretation of what it means to be American in the age of mass incarceration.

The solitary sketched faces, often looking directly along the applicate axis, are reminiscent of the hand-drawn style of forensic facial composites featured in historic wanted posters. Yet, Kolts' portraits subvert the detached style of facial composites and invert the form to create remarkably intimate depictions that are authentic to the voices of the men he sketches. The unity of his sketches with the words written by the depicted inmates offers us greater dimensionality in our encounters with each subject. In drawing a man's eyes, Kolts might amplify the anger or exasperation that the man expresses in his writing. Or he might sketch someone's hands as folded as if in prayer to evoke the subtle humility of the man's writing. Pairing the writings of incarcerated men with Kolts' sketches of them simulates the way that we more intuitively understand other people when we speak to them in person—his portraits give visually perceived authenticity to what the men write.

The collection prioritizes fostering our familiarity with individuals over capturing the scale of mass incarceration. The portraits and anecdotes are relatively limited in number so that we may engage thoughtfully with each person.

A number of themes emerge from the faces and voices that follow. The first section, Indignity, explores the pain and indignities of incarceration, beginning with a sketch of a prison cell so overcrowded that an elderly man sleeps under a table. Urine stagnates mere feet away from the slumbering men. In their anecdotes, the men attest to prison administrators denying them basic medical necessities like insulin and dentures. Others detail the long term effects of prison and the violence constitutive to incarceration on their physicality. Kolts' portraits visualize these horrors for readers: weathered skin, sprawling tattoos, expressionless stares. Though some of the words used by the men in their writing are at least as potent visually as Kolts' sketches: "I was dragged today," begins one man who was violently exiled to solitary confinement: "the HOLE."

The second section, Loss, contemplates the complex interrelation of loss and connection during incarceration. It is bookended by images of men communing with loved ones in the only two ways available to men in prison: over the phone and in visitation rooms. Though these images are on their face about connection, they also serve as representations of how incarcerated people lose unmediated proximity to their loved ones. Connection, in this context, carries the weight of the separation that prison imposes on relationships and families.

Elsewhere in Loss, a man enumerates the events and milestones for his children that he missed while in prison. Another writes a letter to a past lover, sketched next to him by Kolts. In one of several of his poems featured throughout the collection, Roger Deas explores the language of vulnerability and trust—and how its absence robs us of our voice, as experienced by so many in prison.

The third section, Silence, consists of six portraits unaccompanied by text. The symbolism of this section is two-fold. First, the portraits of these men remind us that for every voice of an incarcerated person that we read or hear, there are so many more voices which we will never encounter. Second, silence—or in this case a lack of words—is elusive in prison. Some incarcerated men are drawn to meditation and silent worship practices like Quakerism precisely because they covet silence. There is a basic power and connection that comes from communion unmediated by words. Silence invites us to join in.

The final section, Faith, interrogates existential questions of God, sin, and death. A tongue-in-cheek illustration of a priest trying to save the soul of a dumpster cat who is enjoying a cocktail of discarded "spirits" captures the fraught nature of these topics in prison. One man is shown with his hands folded in prayer, supplicating God for love and light for his family and forgiveness for his sins.

A warrior-poet piloting a wheelchair contemplates fate and the good life in a meandering exposition that acquaints us with his varied philosophical, literary, and artistic inspirations. Faith concludes with a series of vulnerable poems and sketches that reckon with death and the specter of which looms in prison at every turn. Kriss Valerio's moving poem closes the collection with a somber meditation on waiting to die.

This book's central ambition is to acquaint us with the contours of each man's story and the face of he who experienced it. One should move through this collection slowly, lingering awhile as if in conversation. The lives we encounter are varied and complex, difficult but beautiful, and most of all, familiar—vestiges of our flawed pasts, reminders of those whom we love, and perhaps, examples of the precarity of our own futures.

There but for the grace of God go I.

I. Indignity

Incarceration is at its core dehumanizing—an experience antithetical to most any conception of human rights or basic liberty. The question of whether or not that experience is justifiable is distinct from the undeniable reality of prison's ignominy. The first part of the collection, Indignity, is dedicated to the pain inherent to imprisonment and the complicated psychology of those who must endure it.

Indignity begins with a drawing of an overcrowded cell. The central focus of the image is an elderly man lying on a platform on the ground, wedged beneath a table. Our gaze is partially obstructed by two men asleep on bunk beds, indicating the scarcity of space. Clothes and drinkware are strewn around the cell, furthering our perception of the cell's uncleanliness and claustrophobia. In one of the rare instances of color in this collection, yellow urine sits stagnant in the toilet to the side of the beds. A blue blanket and green platform recenter our focus on the cramped man whose sleeping head appears to be mere inches away from the table above him—certain to make any sudden or thoughtless movements painful.

The inspiration for this drawing was a 73 year-old inmate who slept on the floor of his overcrowded cell for more than three months. He was spared worse indignities faced by other men who were forced to sleep on the ground for as long as six months, their heads so close to the toilet that they would wake in the night to the sound and splatter of their cellmates urinating.

The first few pairs of sketches and compositions in Indignity are united by their treatment of the physical effects of incarceration. The poem "Who Cares?" confronts the unnamed writer's own self-described obesity and ugliness and their provenance in his coping with the dejection of prison through excessive eating. The line "My family had enough money for commissary" is laughable in its unexpected simplicity and genuinely moving in its honesty.

His tone grows more sardonic in the final stanza. His fatness, which began as an expression of his waning care for himself and his rehabilitation, becomes a final act of subversion. He envisions a future day when prison staff will struggle to move his unwieldy dead body. He closes his poem with an invidiously honest presumption of how we, the public, think about men like him: forgettable, nameless, and pitiful.

Kolts' accompanying sketch of the poem's author carries the latent anger that fills his words. The man is portrayed in profile, his eyes averting our own gaze. The contours of his face bulge with asymmetry, visualizing the unpleasantness that he asserts about himself in his writing. Crows feet, stretch marks, and creases mar and scrunch his face into a caustic countenance, which in turn amplifies the bitterness of his poetry.

"Animal" and "Just Pete" further evoke a compelling feeling of captivity and desperation. Both sketches are visually softer, even as their words are staggering in their power.

"Animal" is shown with folded hands and closed eyes, as if he is meditating or in prayer, contrasting starkly with his eponymous nickname. His is an image of humility and supplication. The tone of his prose is commensurate: "The treatment I deserve… I do not deserve any sympathy." And yet, it is precisely in his assertion that he looks like an animal and does not deserve sympathy that he appears gentler and elicits our compassion. From that place of moral credibility, he pushes us into discomfort once more: "I am an ANIMAL because I am treated like one."

The author of "Just Pete" is laconic in his writing, telling us plainly the reality he faces on that day. In the simple phrase "I was dragged today," he captures the unadorned horror of the quotidian in prison—of the sudden, uncompromising domination to which inmates are regularly subjected. In Kolts' portrait of him, Pete is marked by subtle shadows around his eyes, lateral face, and shoulders. His austere expression echoes his words.

The mood of accreted through these three pairs culminates with a solitary image titled "Pain," which stands alone without any text. The man portrayed, James, is encircled by a nasal cannula. His face is furrowed with age and blanched by illness. One of his eyes bulges larger than the other, shifting his gaze to be less direct and confrontational. He appears to be suffering, but there is a quiet pride in his endurance that moves us beyond mere pity.

The two other sketches that are unaccompanied by writing in Indignity are "Shaun Humphrey" and "Randall Gebo." "Shaun Humphrey" stares ahead imploringly, his lips tight with consternation. He crosses his arms, revealing an identity bracelet that fetters his right wrist. The bracelet serves as a reminder of both the pervasive surveillance he and the other men are subjected to and the reduction of who they are to a trackable code. Across from "Shaun Humphrey," Kolts depicts "Randall Gebo" with his eyes closed in resignation, seen through thickly framed glasses. His mustache imposes a frown on his otherwise muted expression. "16 ½ to Life | 2nd Degree Murder" is scribbled beneath him, providing jarring context for his imprisonment.

The middle point of Indignity is marked by an illustration of two men gambling over a game of cards, bringing some degree of levity to an otherwise intense series of images and literature. Gambling captures well the moral complexity of so many activities in prison, as it is both a means of casually passing the time socially and an opportunity for potential predation. In the prison environment, nearly every aspect of life carries similar duality.

The remaining pieces featured in Indignity consider how prison imposes upon the health and mental wellbeing of those incarcerated. Kolts' sketch of "Howard Hughes" is one of his most approachable depictions of inmates. His hair is thick and lush, neatly parted, giving him an air of traditional respectability. His square frame glasses and generous but manicured beard and mustache give him a hip aesthetic. He seems conventionally familiar and friendly, perhaps a cousin or neighbor. The feeling of amiability exuded by this image renders Hughes' dramatic writing all the more compelling: all of the sudden, the nice guy from down the street is getting "chained" and "pile[d] into a metal box." He has no idea where he is headed—just that he is leaving his current facility on a few minutes notice. We're left feeling a sliver of his disorientation, and a rush of anger over what seems like a senseless display of arbitrary power.

"Preston Foster" and "Dave Allen" describe disturbing instances of neglect in which prison officials ignored their basic health care needs. "Preston Foster" writes with considerable restraint for a man who had his dentures taken by prison officials for several months. Kolts depicts him with his mouth closed and his eyes looking forward somberly. The frames of his glasses obscure his gaze, softening what might otherwise be a more biting stare. He has overgrown sideburns and a balding head that signify the humility of middle age. He doesn't look angry—mostly sad. He wants his teeth, and to be able to take care of his dying wife. Yet, prison denies him both.

"Dave Allen" is a threnody to the American Dream in the age of mass incarceration. He chronicles his humble but dignified family-man past, cut short by his arrest and denial of bail. The years he spends in jail before his trial compromises his diabetes, leading to episodic health scares that leave him and his family in fear. In the accompanying sketch, "Dave Allen" is stoic. A medical mask is pulled down below his chin, reminding us of the heightened precarity that communicable diseases present to people who have myriad health challenges. The shadows around his eyes express his fatigue.

The final pairings in Indignity immerse us in the illogical and incoherent realities of prison. "Cliff Johnson" recounts a meandering phantasmagoria of shadow people, spider webs, and bright blue skies. He appears weathered in his sketch, with eyes that carry a certain laconic wisdom suggesting he does not ramble in his words—though he might indulge theatricality in his writing. Meanwhile,

"Cody Coburn" writes in a more taciturn style compared to "Cliff Johnson." His syntax is terse and coarse, cycling through subjects abruptly after only sparing details. Yet, there is a simple rhythm to his writing that brings a skeletal coherence to what seems to be almost impenetrable at certain points. The accompanying sketch of "Cody Coburn" is one of the few portraits in which the subject's face is not shown. Instead, he is seen moving about in a cafeteria, fixated on the food before him, in stark contrast with the blunt vulnerability of his writing.

Indignity closes with an iconoclastic sketch of "Justice in Vermont." An imperious judge sneers at us, his arms fraternally embracing a public defender and a prosecutor. Each attorney carries a briefcase inscribed with their respective positions in tiny letters, juxtaposed with larger, bold letters that reminds us that both work for the State. The attorneys' mouths hang open with demeaning laughter as they stand above the scales of justice weighing in favor of a pile of cash over "no evidence." The courts, perhaps more than prisons themselves, garner the near universal ire of inmates.

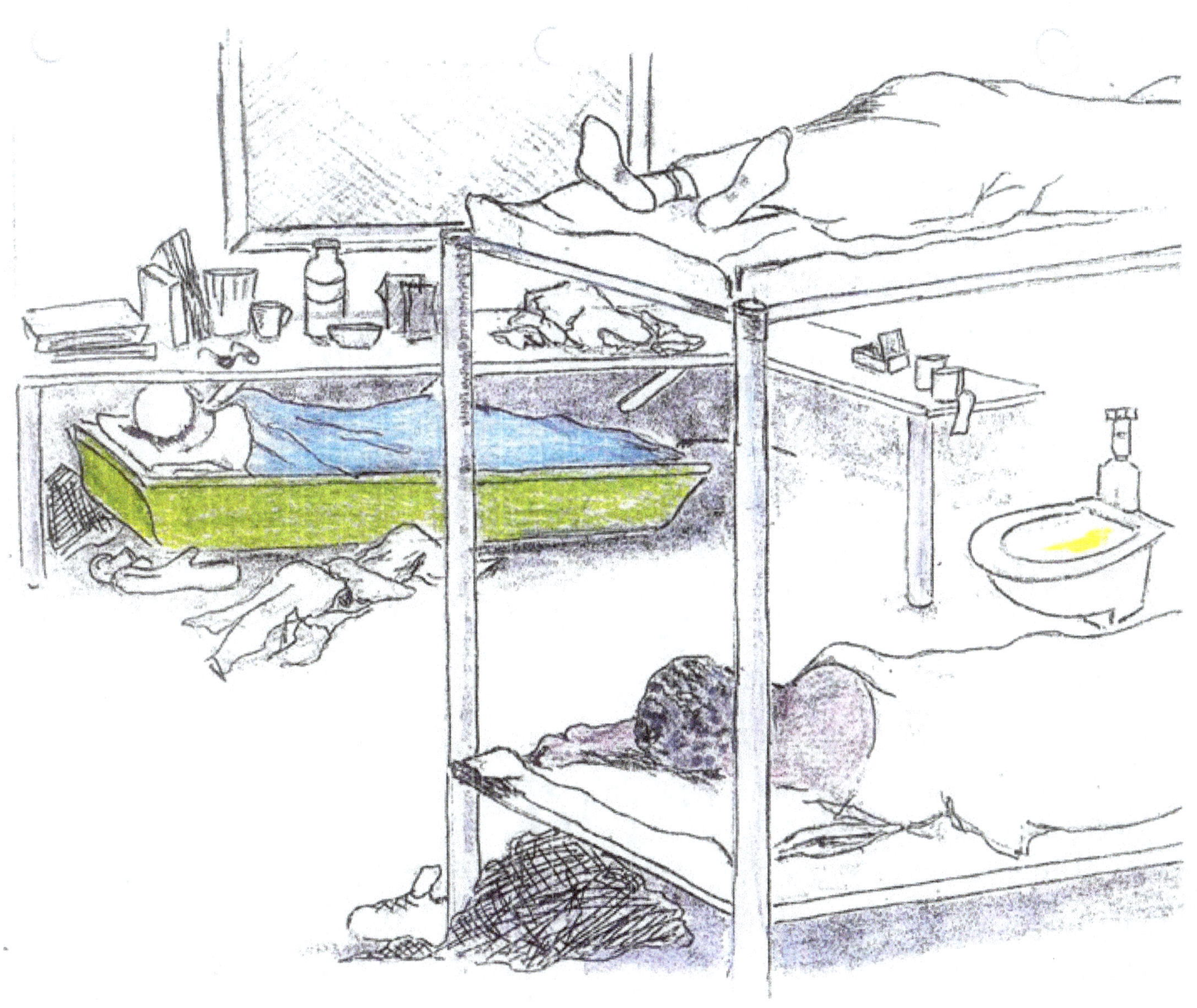

Who Cares?

I hesitated to contribute.
I think you can see why. Yeah, I know,
I'm ugly.
But it wasn't always that way.
When I came in some 20 years ago, I cared!
But as years went by and the parole
board kept denying my release, I knew
I would never get out.
Food became my friend.
My family had enough money for my commissary.

I just don't care.
There is just this lie about rehabilitation
and getting out,
But, no one cares.

So, I just eat and secretly laugh about how
hard it will be to remove my body
when I finally die
How perverse is that?
You don't need to know
My name— hardly anyone does—
but remember my face—
it will be in the obituary soon,
and you will say—
POOR FAT GUY

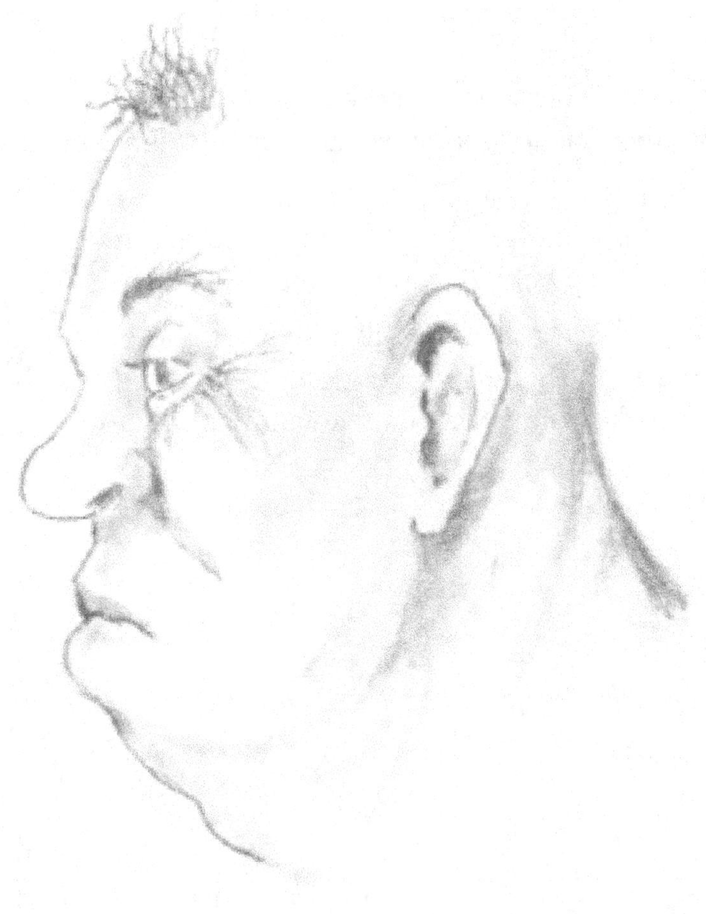

Animal

This is the face of a failed man, who has been battered by the prison system in Vermont for as long as I can remember. Made to look like an animal so much that the inmates began to call me just that: Animal.

I lost my family and children, and I suffer in misery and pain. I get no relief or reprieve. I am just a number hidden away behind concrete and barbed wire.

The treatment I deserve, because that is what the State promises you, the public. And the agonies I endure please the State. I do not deserve any sympathy, because I have done my wrongs to be exiled here. But make no mistake: I am an animal because I am treated like one.

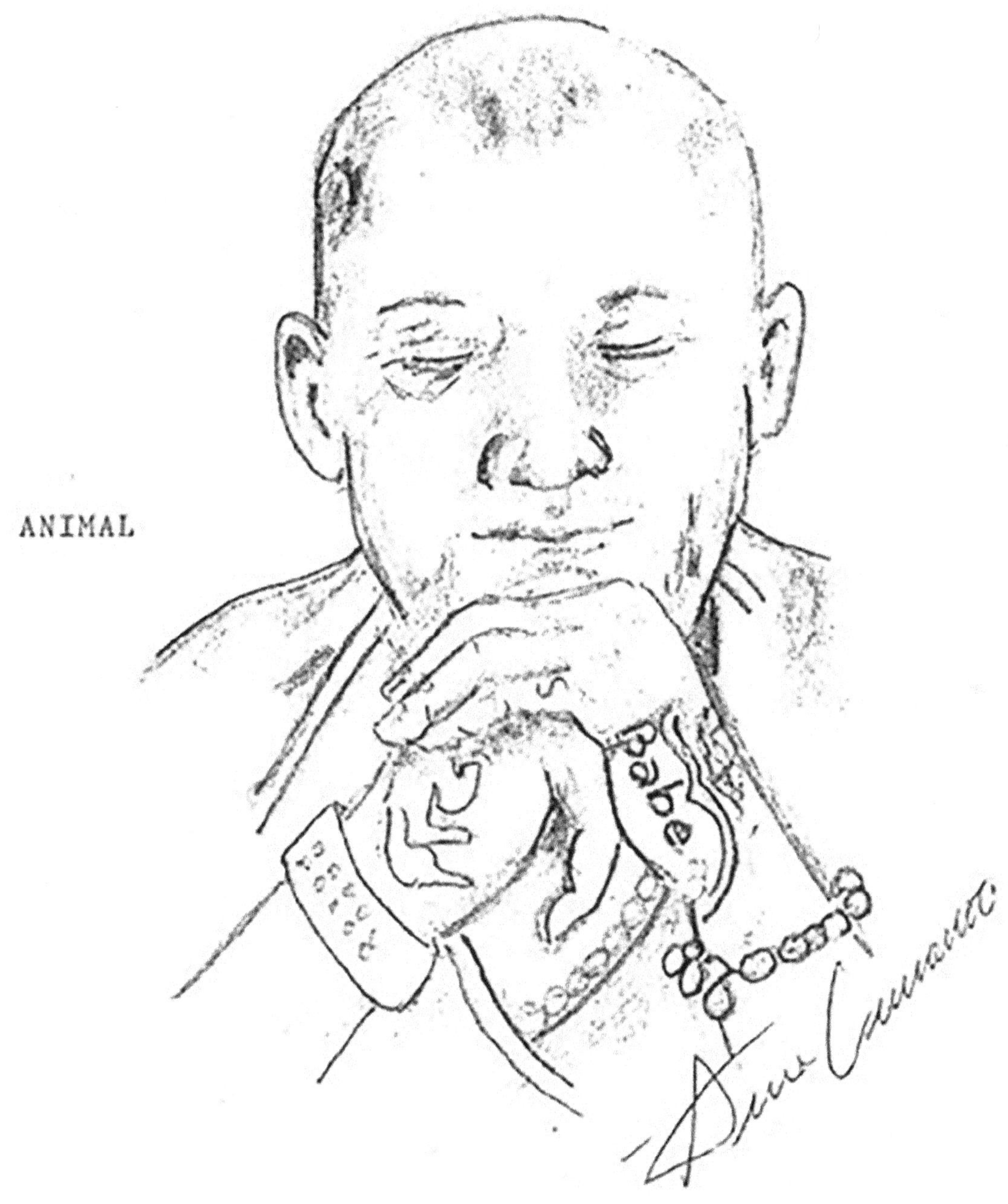

ANIMAL

Just Pete

I was dragged today.

They tell me I need to be in protective custody, for what reasons I am not sure.

But that part doesn't matter—the facility determines the appropriate remedy, not me.

To the "hole"

I expect to be there for at least a few days.

I grieve. Things happen so quickly here.

Unintentionally? There are no exceptions.

Hope for the best.

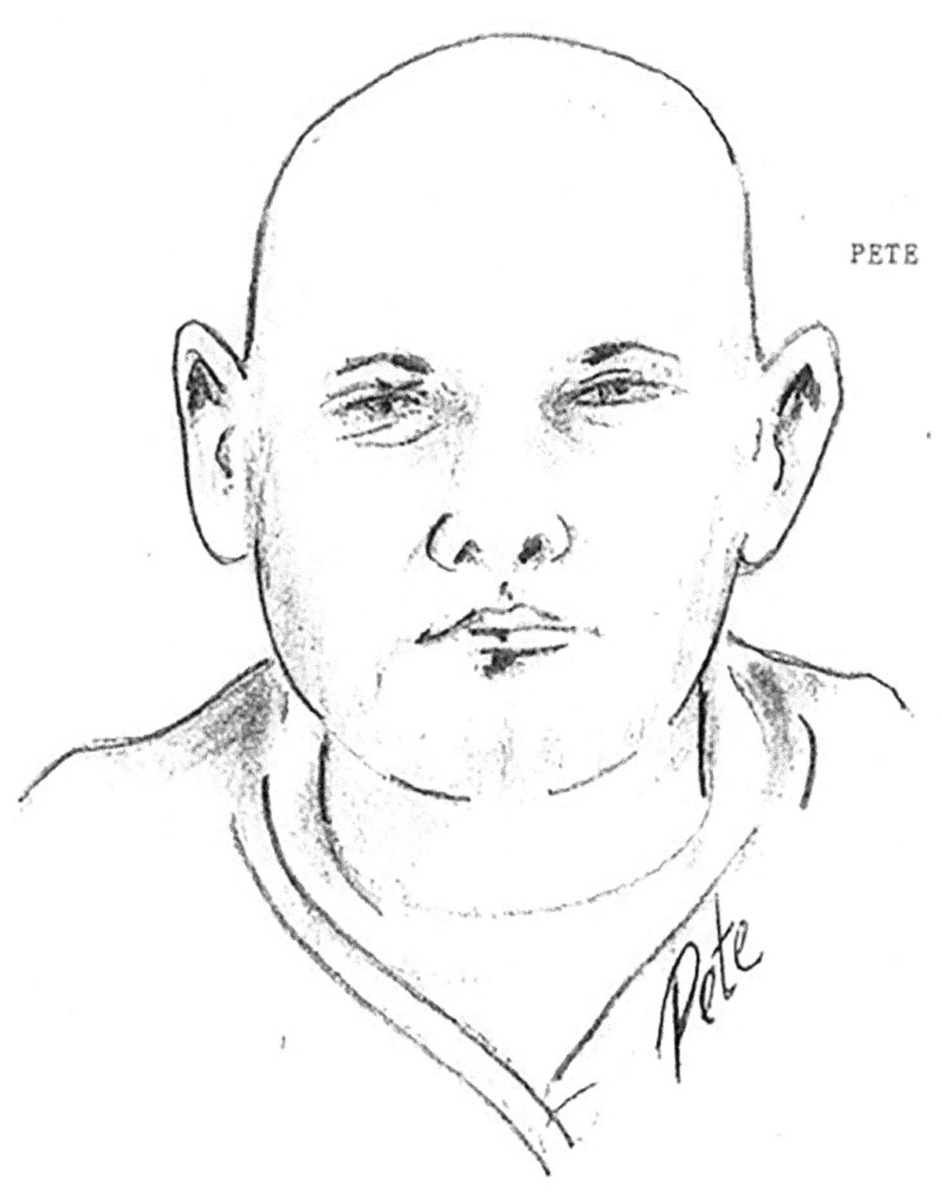

PETE
Pete

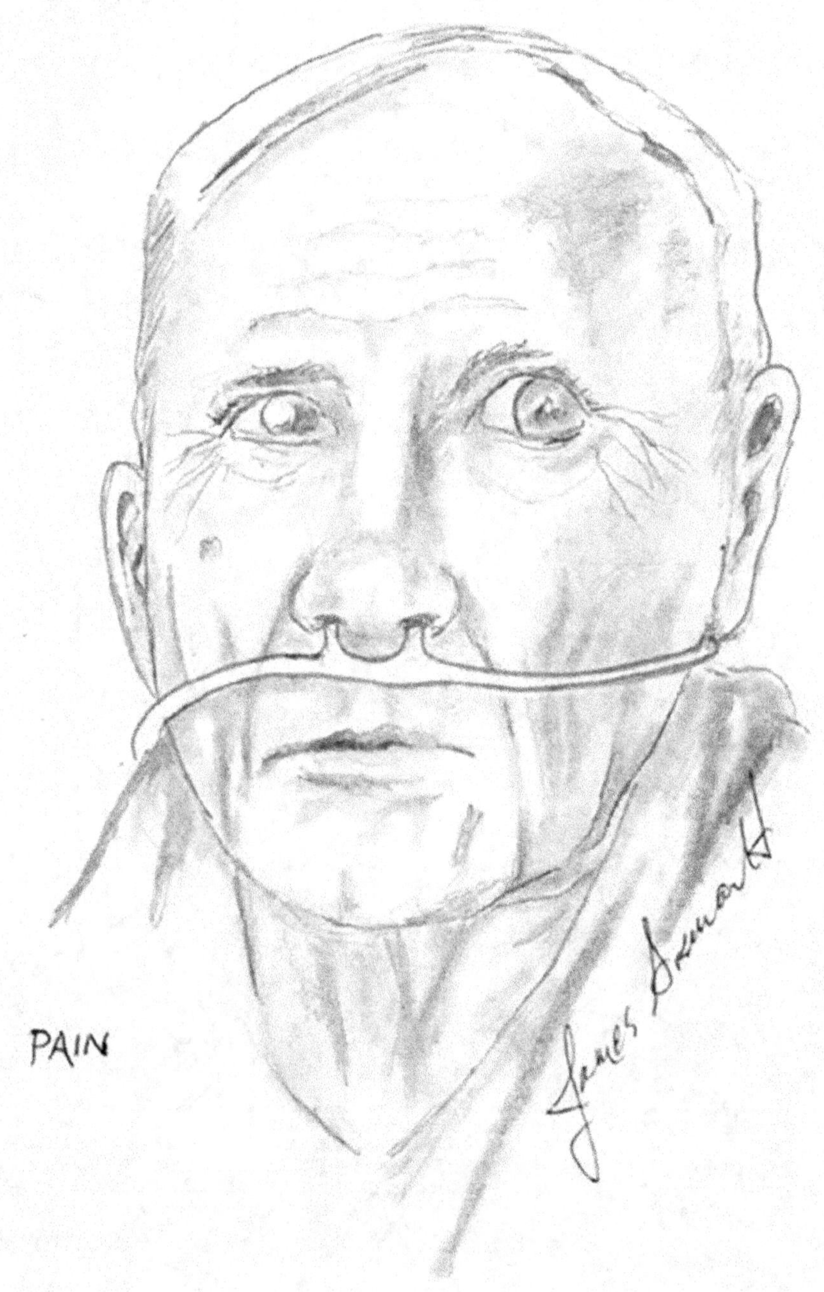

PAIN
James Stewart

GAMBLING

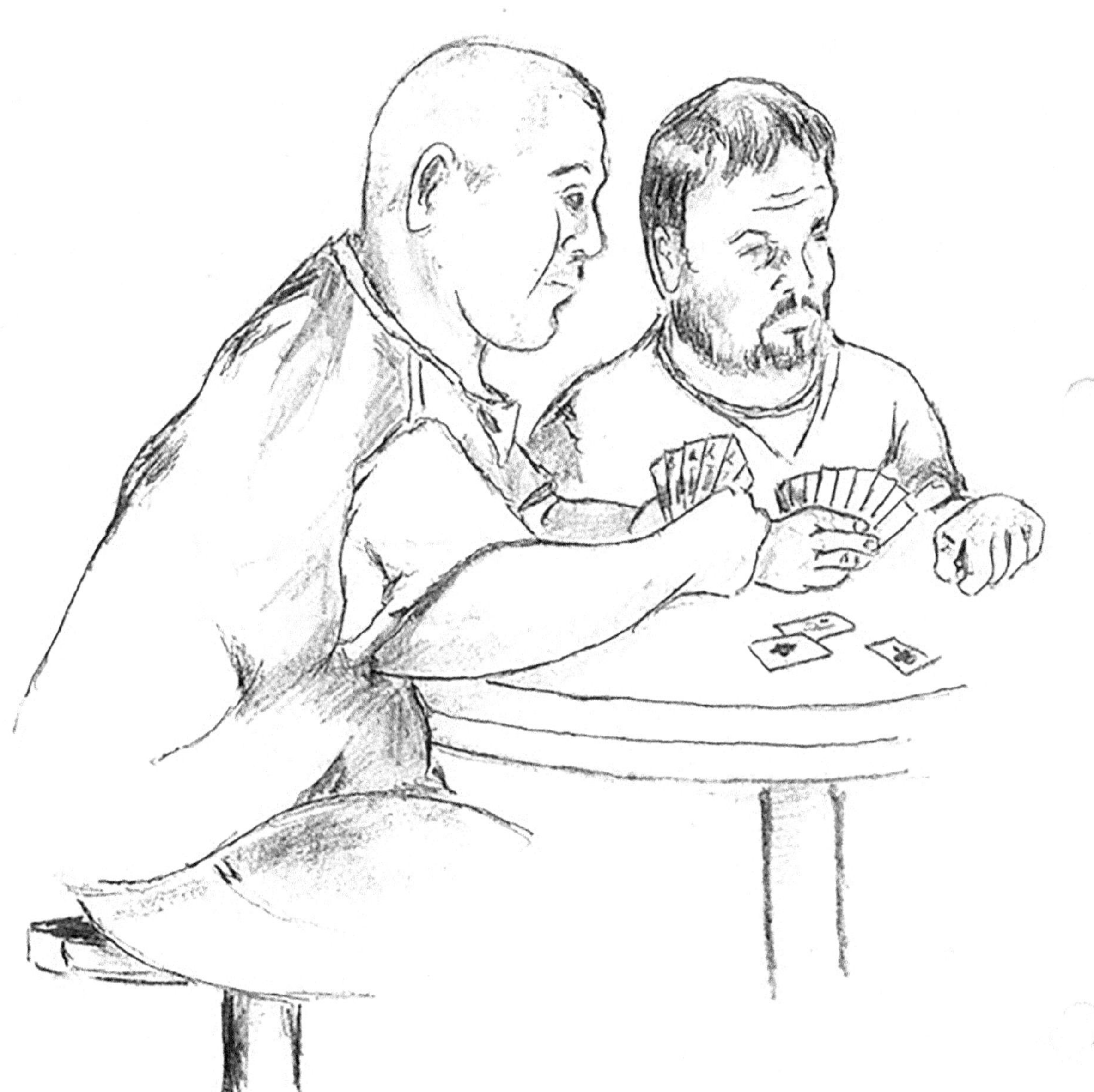

Howard Hughes

I'm in a rush. Just got word I am being shipped to another facility.

Shipping is instant, literally a few minutes to pack up all your belongings in a plastic bag, and get ready to be shipped. There is no preparation, and you must adjust immediately. You barely have time to say "so long" to whatever friends you might have made. Get ready, get chained, "legs and hands please!" Pile into a metal box and hope for the best, because when you are loaded, you don't know where you are going.

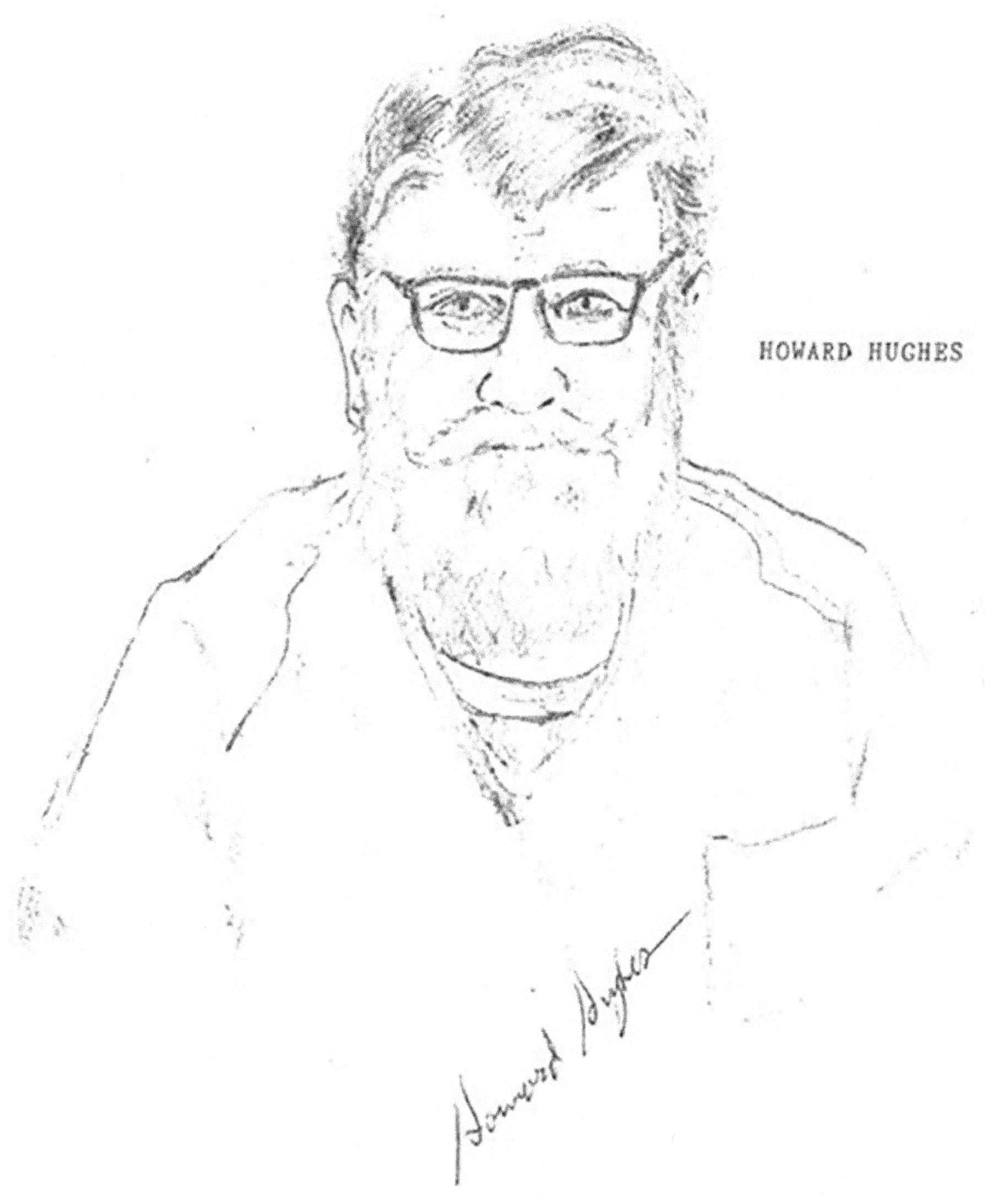

15

Preston Foster

They took my teeth a few months ago.

I went nuts after they overmedicated me a few weeks into my stint at the jail in Rutland. They maced me and shipped me to Springfield in a suicide smock with no clothes, none of my stuff—and no dentures! The shackles cut up my ankles, my shoulders are bruised. I still had marks after four months.

That was more than six months ago. Still no teeth.

My wife has it worse though. She's got Stage 4 bone cancer and has about two years to live. Her condition gets worse every time we talk. And I'm not there to take care of her. I'm trying to cut a deal to get out on probation or furlough or house arrest or whatever I can get to be able to take care of my wife. But that takes time. Something she doesn't have much of.

And I'm still fighting for my teeth.

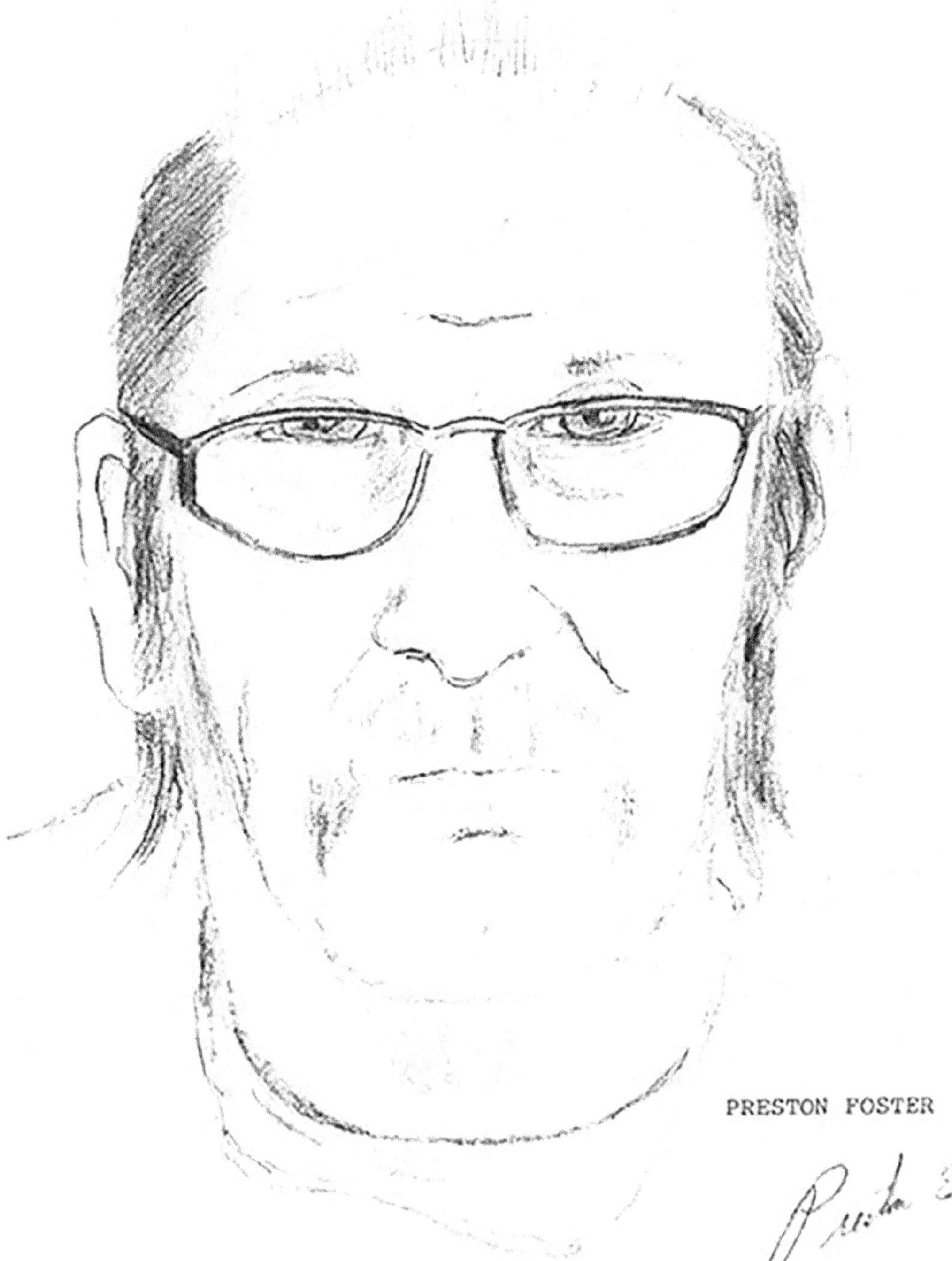

PRESTON FOSTER

Dave Allen

My arrest happened one summer night in front of my toddler daughter. The prosecutor argued I was a danger to the community and I was denied bail. I've sat in jail for more than two years waiting for my trial.

I worked most of my life in the entertainment industry. Before my arrest, I had a good job at an inn owned by an Ivy League college, earning enough of a living to support two children and two stepchildren. I taught Sunday school at my church, drummed for the worship band, and filled in for the pastor whenever he was away.

As a family, we valued service. We spent Thanksgiving serving the homeless and needy. During Christmas time, I volunteered as a Santa Claus at department stores. Everywhere I went, I tried to bring smiles, laughter, hope and joy.

I lived the American dream.

Now, I'm fighting for my life behind bars. When I lived a stable life, it was easy for me to maintain my health despite the challenges posed by my diabetes. Here, I have little control of my medical care. People don't usually think about that aspect of prison—giving up your right to make decisions about your health.

The prison won't even give me the device I need to manage my blood sugars. My levels spike and flood me with pain, with little I can do about it. It's torture. Sometimes, my blood sugar crashes so low that I black out or have seizures, putting me at the mercy of my fellow inmates to find me help. But nothing changes. My health still hangs in the balance.

So much for that American dream.

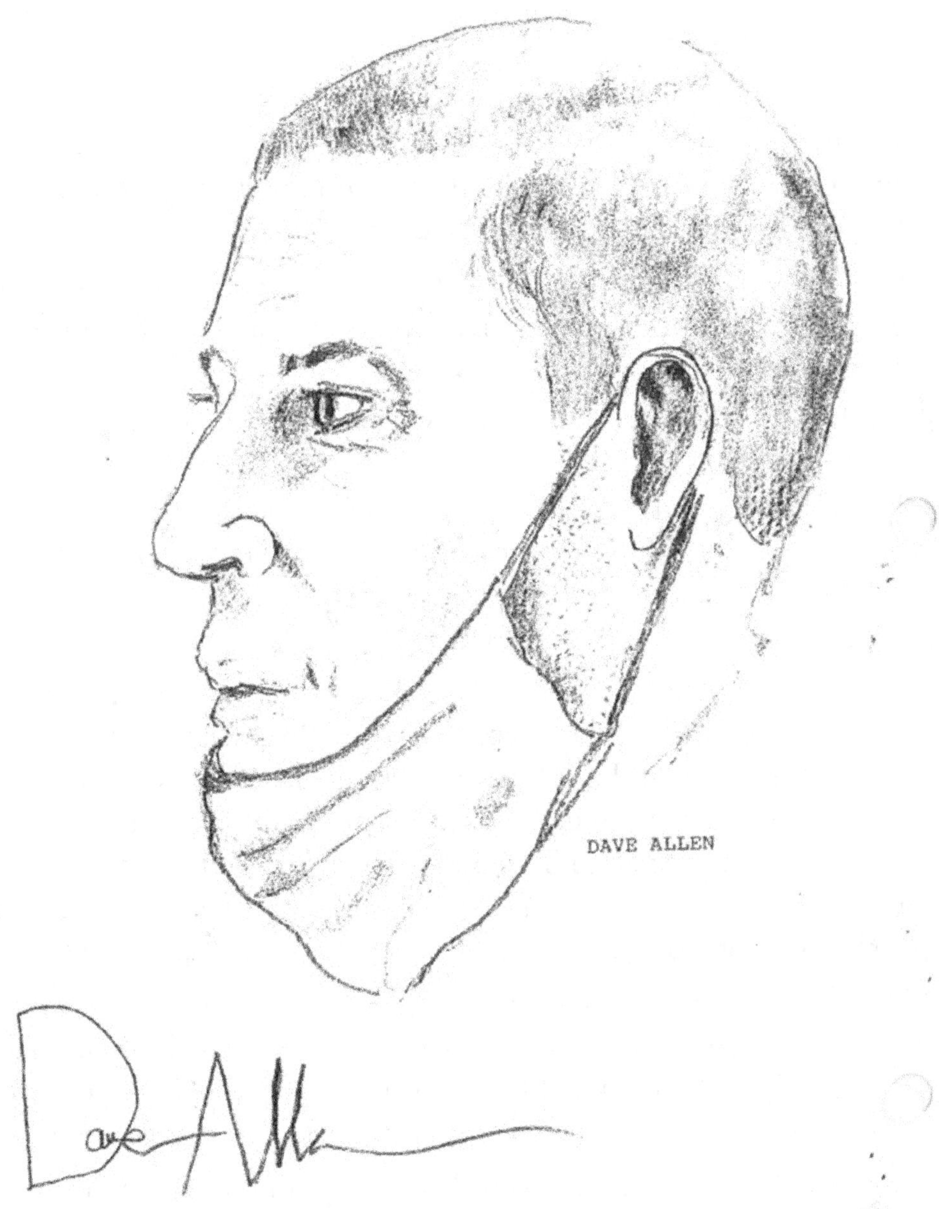

19

Cliff Johnson

Clouds are getting darker as they move slowly across the vast sky. I am bored, really bored. No T.V. for four and a half days, and of course there is no hurry to get the line repaired and back on. It's days like this that your thoughts turn to the dark side.

Nothing is looking good ahead of the day. Dark clouds, no sun, dampness in the air we are breathing. Can't go outside, too much construction going on and of course everything has a cloak of secrecy about it.

Oh, look to the sky! There is a hole in the sky—nice piece of blue sky just for me. It looks to be the right size for my body to go through. What am I thinking? I know my body is just a spirit when I pass. I am told my brain lives on an extra little when I pass. An extra thirty minutes until the body stops functioning. I guess I have some unfinished business. My brain is racing to end the run—however for 81 years it has a lot of catchup to do.

Just came in from the outside and it is beautiful—a wonderful blue sky, with clouds looking as if they were cotton balls floating in the sky. I saw from the corner of my eyes little shadow people. They headed in my direction, and I ran as fast as I could but they were much faster than I. I am stopped in my tracks as I look at the side of a brick building— a very large shadow gets closer and closer and bigger and bigger. As I tremble, I see the headlights of a vehicle, and it's getting closer to me. This must be my last day on earth. I heard a gunshot from my backside and then another, while there standing in a puddle of oil. I just can't move. My neck sways left and right trying to watch the action around me. Coming from nowhere, a large spider web appears. As the web gets tighter, the two legged spider stands erect giving me a glance.

That shadow on the building is just standing still forever. A third shot rings out and ricochets from building to building. All of a sudden a big bang—the shadow gets smaller. All around the web—sticky. It is quiet as we try to loosen from this sticking mess we are in.

A voice from afar begs to be freed from this web, from the stuff which sticks us in place.

THIS IS WHAT INCARCERATION WILL DO TO YOU

TO ME!

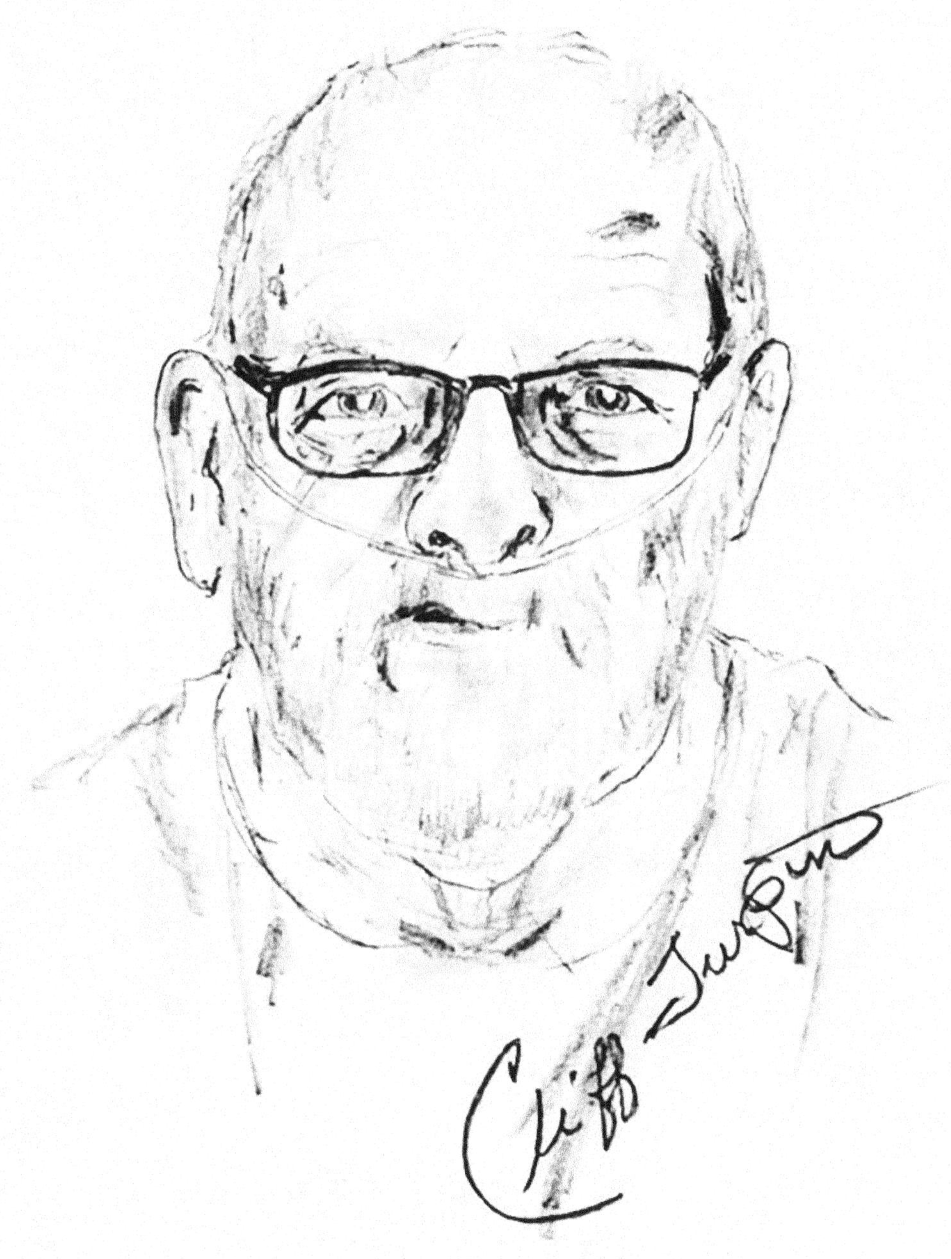

21

Cody Coburn

Renegade. Want to do programs. Six weeks past minimum then get out. Can't do paperwork from bad to good behavior with no reporting. Got into a fight—kicked out of a group which cost me 20 months. Other guy came back in 30 days.

Pick and choose who to prosecute. Wait twelve months to get back in—two weeks past the end of programming while everyone else gets out.

No one knows until bad things happen.

Bargaining, plea agreement, programming—all tools to keep you in check.

Relief, pacing in your pod.

Programming is only in Newport and Springfield. Relief, pacing in jail.

Some people want to put this behind them, while some people embrace it and continue their path.

It is hard for the people that actually want to change in this environment.

Fight, well you go to the hole.

They fuck with the guys who are on programming because they can get away with it. Can't get in trouble here or out there.

Does any of this make sense? Neither does prison.

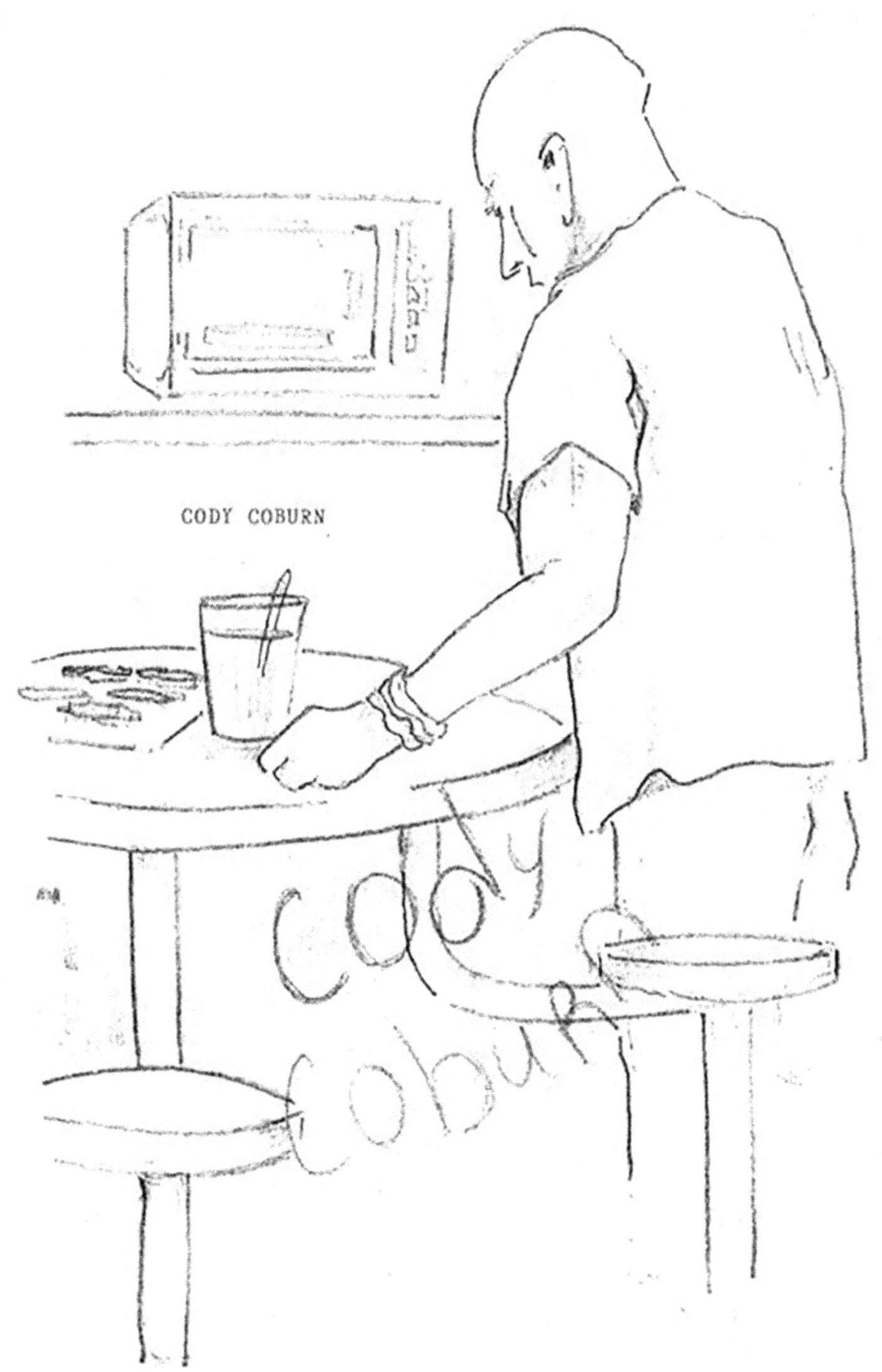
CODY COBURN

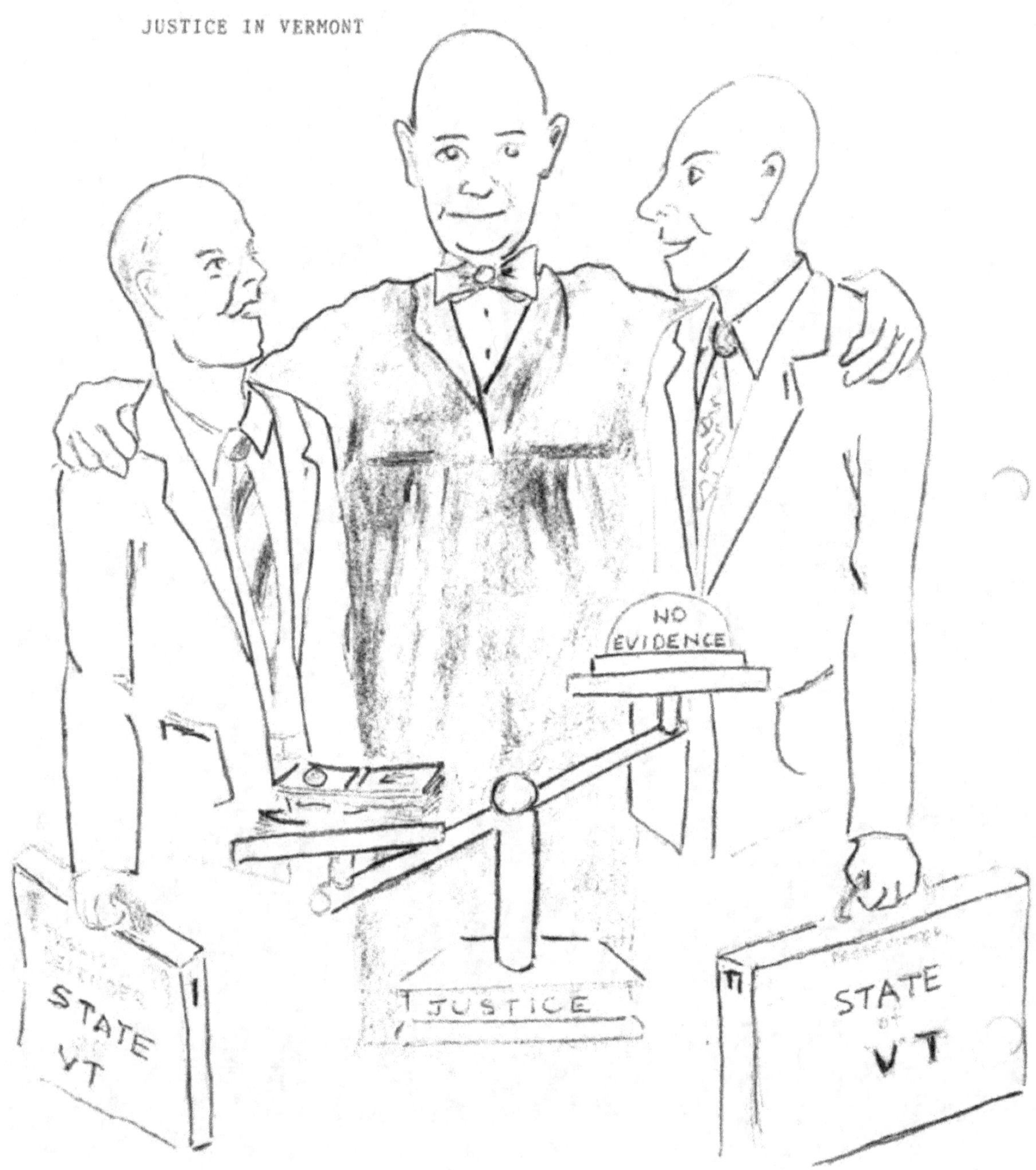

NO EVIDENCE
STATE VT
JUSTICE
STATE OF VT

II. Loss

Prison takes far more than someone's freedom: family, lovers, community, jobs, homes—time. The losses mount. Loss is a collection that interrogates the stakes of prison in terms of what people must give up, often forever, when they are held captive there. The portraits and writings of this section are contextualized with two images at the beginning and end that uniquely portray loss through what seems to be its opposite: connection. Phone calls and visits are the only ways that people in prison are allowed to connect with some of the people whom they have lost. Yet, that mediated connection is also a reminder of their separation. The harsh realities of prison phone calls and visitations strip away the idealized perception of these privileges as wholly positive.

In Kolts' illustration of the phone room, all three booths are occupied, signifying both the enthusiastic use of the service by inmates as well as its scarcity. In many cases, there are as few as three phones to service over fifty inmates, creating long wait times during high demand periods like holidays. Inmates receive minimal privacy—even during legal calls—from each other or from correctional officers. The frustrating imposition of correctional officers is represented comically in the sketch by a uniformed man looking into a mirror nearby: a clown face stares back at him. The illustration of a woman and child visiting a man in the final image of the section, there too a clown-faced officer watches the intimate exchange off to the side. Inmates wait for weeks, months, or even years to see family members—only to have to share those moments with other inmates or officers. Surveillance, and the way in which it distracts and detracts from the intimacy of visits from loved ones, is at the heart of this piece.

The separation imposed on prisoners and their loved ones is not always at the root of loss. Stigma, judgment, and the impact of an inmate's crime often drives people away. "Leonard and Pamela" expresses the heartbreak that results when a lover walks away from someone in prison. Leonard and Pamela are sketched side by side, their heads tenderly touching one another's. Pamela smiles warmly, but signs of fatigue—whether from her own struggles or her partner's—crack through around her eyes and mouth. A thickly mustached Leonard poses with the plain expression of detached masculinity. His affection is quietly revealed only through the slight tilt of his head into Pamela's. Pamela's head is framed in shades of blue and purple that mask her neck and shoulders, giving her a spectral quality that corresponds with her disappearance from Leonard's life. "Pamela stopped believing in me," Leonard says of her absence with crushing honesty, testifying to one of the most devastating sentiments that can be expressed to someone in prison. His words drip with resignation, but he still insists—even futilely—that he loves Pamela: "I still love you. Your man, Leonard."

Losing love is central to "Ronnie D. Spears" as well. Ronnie Spears cycled through the justice systems of New York and Vermont for more than three decades, starting at fifteen years old. He speaks passingly of his kids, but he lingers on their mother—"I love her. I gave her up a long time ago, but I miss her." In his portrait, we see him in profile with his eyes scrunched faintly as if he is straining to catch a glimpse of his former lover in the distance.

When faced with losing free access to family and other loved ones, someone threatened with imprisonment is often willing to make compromises to get out as quickly as possible. The daunting stakes of prison lead to roughly ninety-five percent of people charged with crimes to accept plea deals—that is, agreements with a prosecutor to plead guilty to a crime in exchange for a lesser sanction. This complicated phenomenon, and the impact that someone's lost time with their families can have on it, is the focus of "Matt Roberts." Matt Roberts takes account of the milestones in his children's lives he's missing while in prison to offer context for why he would accept "that 4-letter word," a plea, instead of fighting to prove his innocence. His portrait furthers his image as a young father doing his best. He averts his eyes to the side in a humble gesture. His goatee and raunchy tattoo revealed by his sleeveless shirt give him a casualness and approachability that echoes the uncomplicated sincerity of his writing and his intentions to get back to his family no matter the sacrifice he must make himself.

Both "Richard A. West" and "Vladimir Augustov" account for their losses in the most straightforward terms: time. The sketch of Richard West depicts him holding a card that reads "23 ½" to represent the half of his life that he has spent behind bars for a litany of crimes since 1986. He is optimistic though: he gets out of prison soon, and never plans to come back. Vladimir Augustov is less optimistic. Convicted of sexually assaulting a child, Vladimir Augustov has spent decades in prison, and he was sent back not long after he got out the first time. He questions the logic of his continued incarceration, citing the steep cost to the state to keep him behind bars. "When will it be enough?" he asks us. In the accompanying sketch, he glares at us over the top of his rectangular glasses. His forehead furrowed and his lips clenched tightly, he looks skeptical and irascible. But his eyes hold greater complexity. The brow above his left eye cuts downwards angrily. His right eye, however, is softer, with a relaxed brow that evokes greater vulnerability. Though these expressions seem contradictory, their combination captures the way guilt, coercion, and captivity entangle unlike emotions. He is guarded but vulnerable; exasperated but repentant.

Entangled emotions are central to the perspective of "Todd J. Hemingway." He locks his eyes onto our own, but his expression is not confrontational. There is an honesty in his directness, emphasized further by the Christian cross that hangs around his neck. And in that honesty, he shares his thoughts on one of the most controversial questions an inmate can ponder: are they better off in prison? "Less stress, no bills. No one to send you back in," he offers us for our own consideration. We wonder, is this a flippant thought? A sign of Stockholm syndrome? Or might it hold some truth? And if it does, what does that say of our society's failures and shortcomings?

Each pair in Loss compounds the sense of isolation caused by imprisonment and the connections that inmates most forfeit. Roger Deas' poem, "WORDS," encapsulates these losses and distills them down to the basic currency of connection: language. He parlays language's role in connection to raise the question of "the power of the spoken word" in the opposite—disconnection. He warns "you can crush a soul for life" so "consider carefully what comes from your lips." In the context of how much people in prison have lost, Roger Deas implores us to consider if our additional judgment—our words—serve any worthy purpose.

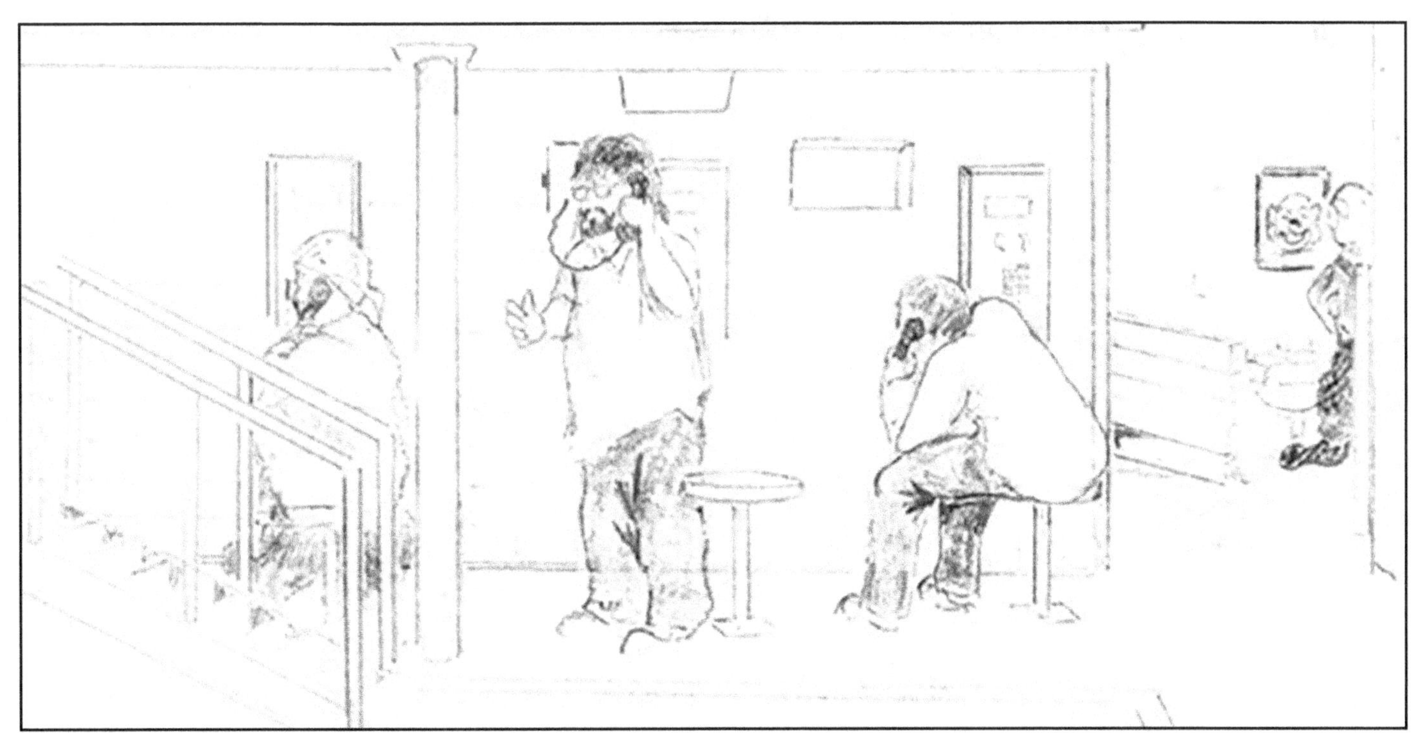

Leonard and Pamela

I haven't seen or heard from Pamela since January 15, 2019, when my life turned upside down. We had just gotten a new place together. Then, my life went downhill. Betrayed by my own brother, my parole officer took me away.

Pamela stopped believing in me, and hasn't talked to me since.

I have tried to have family members get in touch with her—just to get some news. I hope to know something before I get out in another year.

Pam, you know where I am and that I still love you.

Your man, Leonard

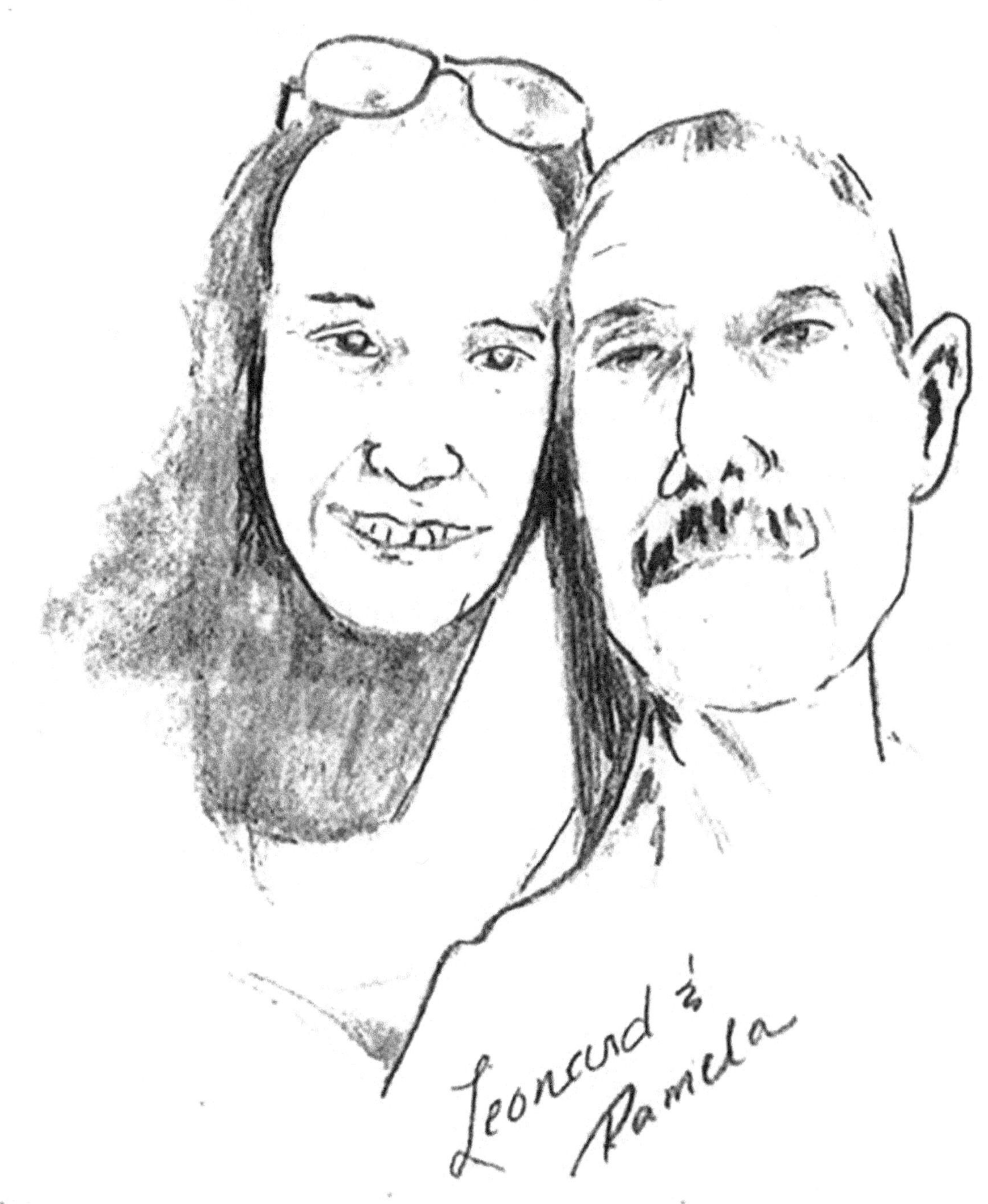

Leonard &
Pamela

Ronnie D. Spears

I have been in and out of the system since, well, since I was 15 years old. That was 33 years ago.

I've got two kids. A daughter with special needs. My baby's mother, I love her. I gave her up a long time ago, but I still miss her.

I'm in Vermont now, but I'm originally from the South Bronx, N.Y. Vermont is a good place, with a lot of good people, but the law has been hard on me.

Don't know what else to say!

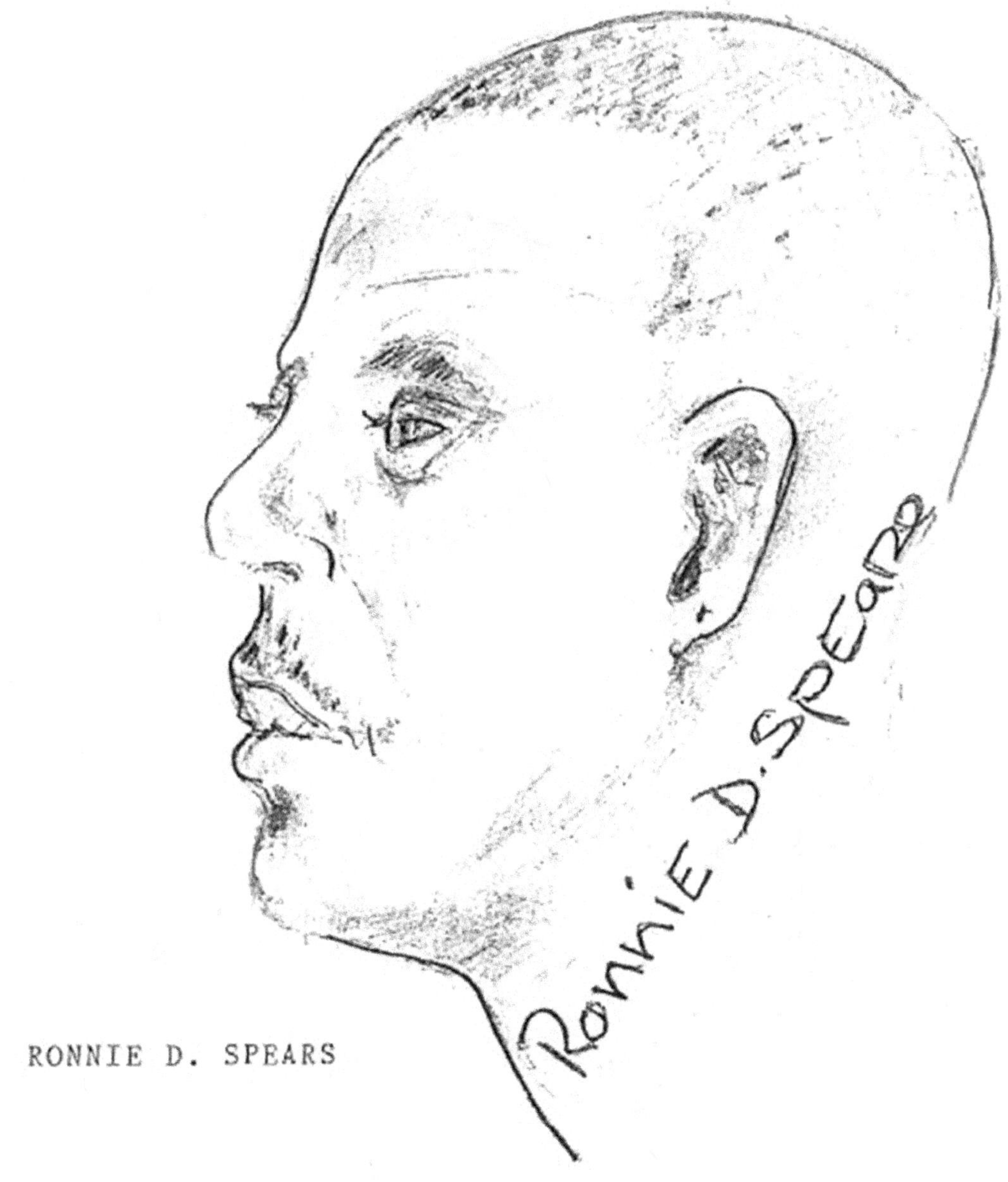

RONNIE D. SPEARS

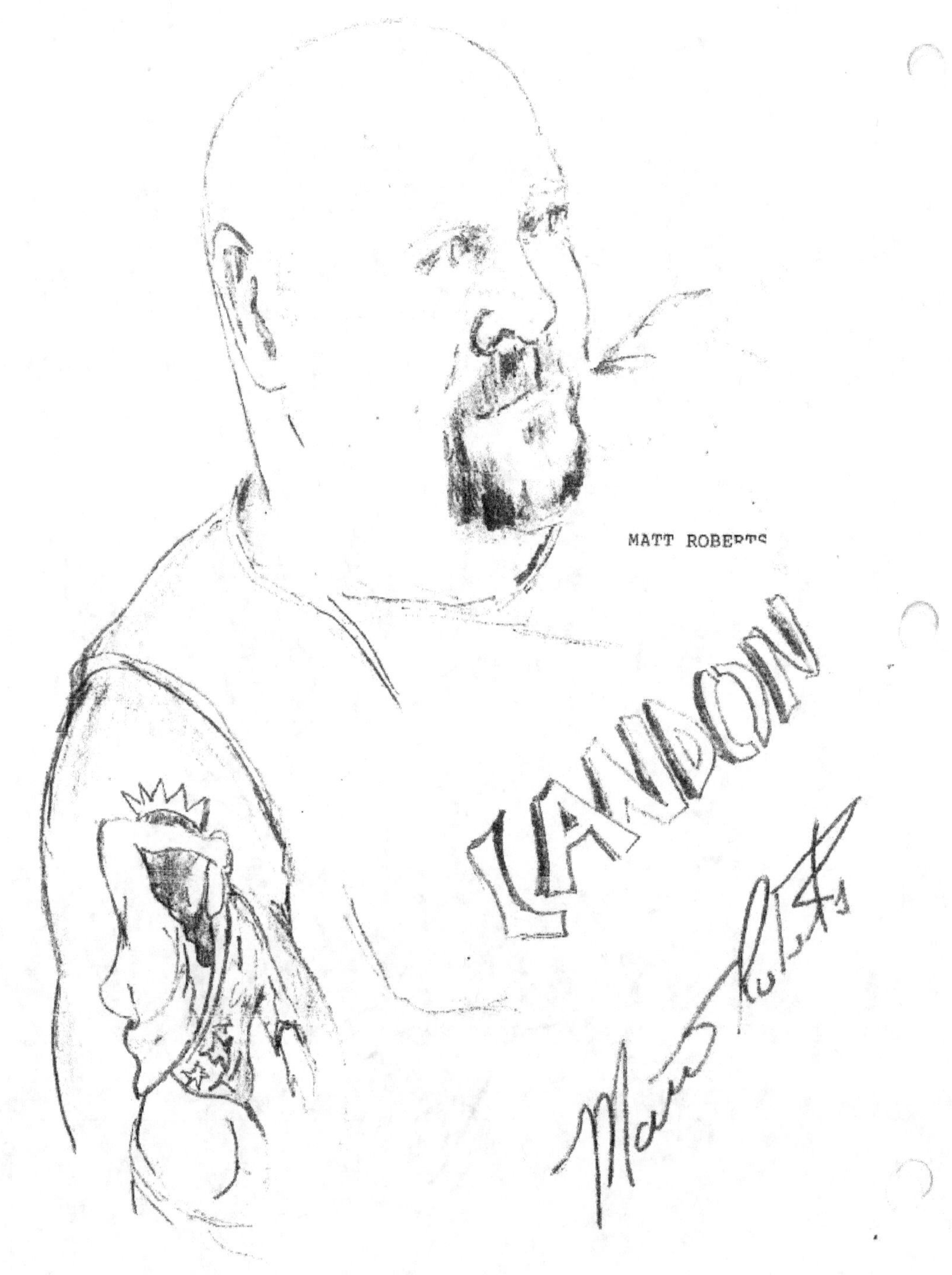

MATT ROBERTS
LANDON

Matt Roberts

I have been incarcerated since May 2021. This is my first time I have been in trouble with the law. This has been a life altering experience for me.

First and foremost, I'm a father of the two most amazing kids in this world. There is nothing more important to me than family.

Since my first day being incarcerated, I have had to adapt to a world I know nothing about, people of whom I don't know, and a lifestyle I know nothing about.

Doing time on someone else's schedule the way they want. This is hard for me, being a hard-working man that runs a crew of people, coming and going as I please at any time.

I have lost so much time with my family. My family whom I've never been absent from, my children, missing my daughter's high school graduation, her 18th birthday. Almost losing my son in a motorcycle accident. My son's 16th birthday, school events, JROTC, Color Guard, sports. Not to forget the holidays, have all been a huge struggle for myself and my children.

Being in jail with charges against me that threaten my very freedom, for what could be the rest of my life. So, I work with my public defender trying to get released to "Responsible Adults" so I can be a part of the very life I miss so much.

But after numerous attempts I was denied my freedom. So now after almost a year in jail I'm taking a plea. I was denied my chance to go home until that 4-letter word came into play.

I'm taking charges that I will hold for life, to return to my children, my family, where I truly belong.

Richard A. West

I am 48 years old. I've spent every bit of half of my life behind bars: 23 years and six months. My criminal history started back in 1986 and went straight through to the present day. Driving under the influence, aggravated assault, fraud, robbery—I've done it all.

I will finally max out my sentence in 20 days, at the beginning of summer. I will be leaving jail for the final time of my life, I am sure!

Never to return.

I don't have regrets. I've learned a lot in jail.

But I still don't recommend it.

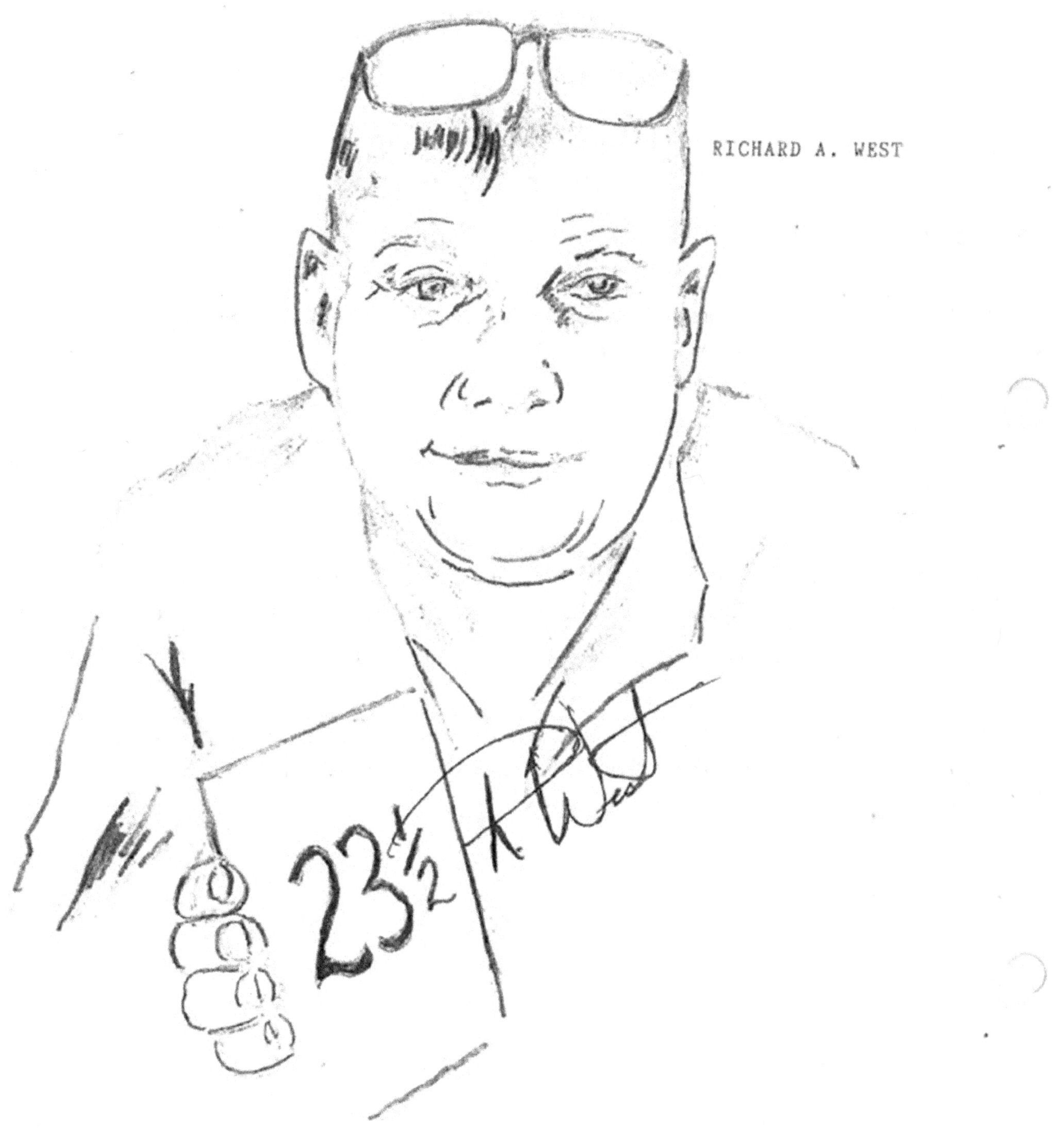

35

Vladmir Augustov

I came from Russia to the United States to perform in circuses in 1991. For fifteen years, I brought joy to children.

Until I didn't. In 2006, I touched someone who was underage. I admitted to my horrible crime. I was convicted, sentenced, and imprisoned.

I've been out of prison once, for 14 months. All I wanted was to see the circus again. I rode my bicycle down to Shelburne Farms, but I didn't think to tell my parole officer that I was going to the show. I was working at a Burger King so I was around children every day. But they thought the circus was different.

My parole officer arrested me and I lost my apartment. Since I didn't have a place to go back to, they threw me in jail rather than let me out on bail. My caseworker told me about another inmate who chose to be deported rather than stay here. She suggested I consider it. I declined.

I had a job, a place to live, and remorse for my crimes—I was getting my life back together. Gone, in an instant.

Now, I am 69 years old. Still here for what I did decades ago. I've paid a steep price for my actions, and the State has paid a steep price for my actions as well: to date, $910,000 to keep me behind bars.

When will it be enough?

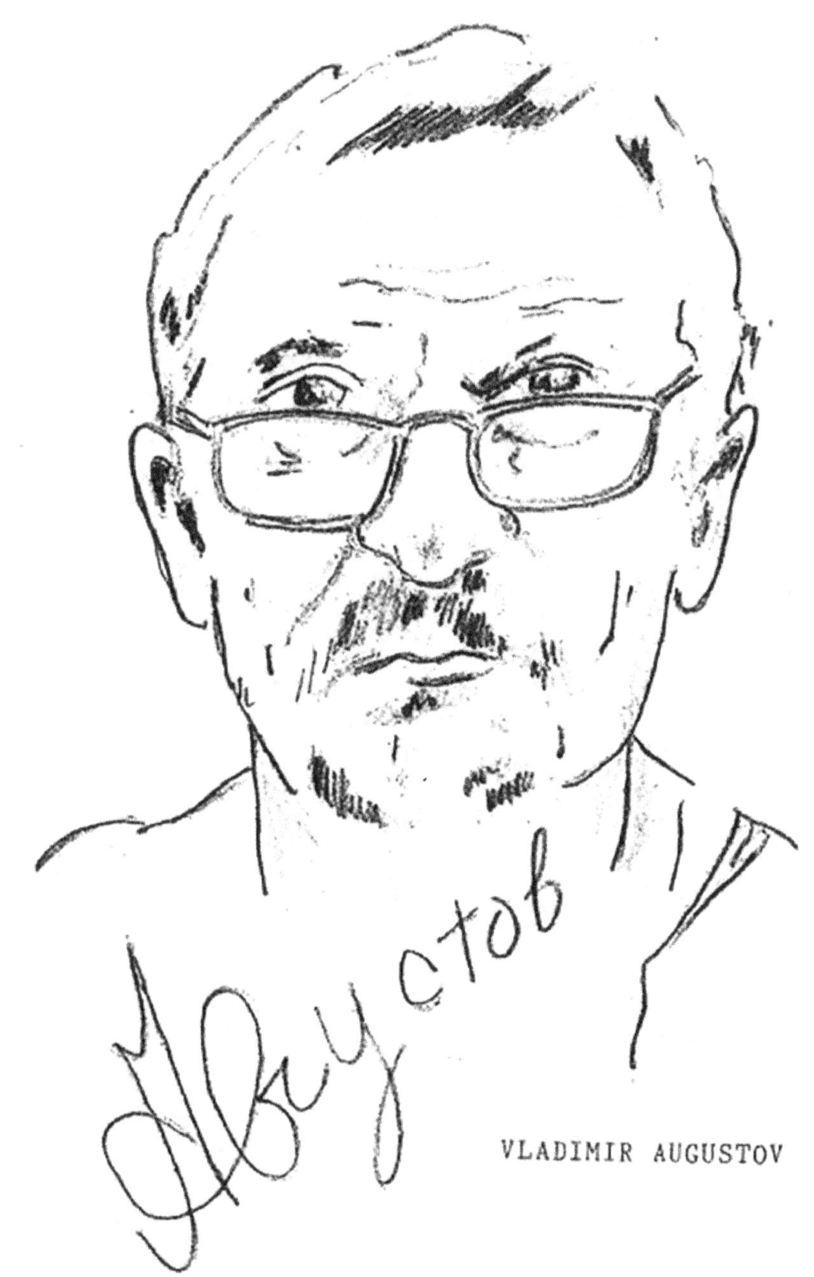

VLADIMIR AUGUSTOV

Todd J. Hemingway

I miss my family. But sometimes it feels as though it is safer here than out there. Less stress, no bills. No one to send you back in. Not everyone here is a bad person—they just made the wrong decision in difficult times. I have had enough, finally. So many wasted years here: in and out, in and out. For all the wrong reasons.

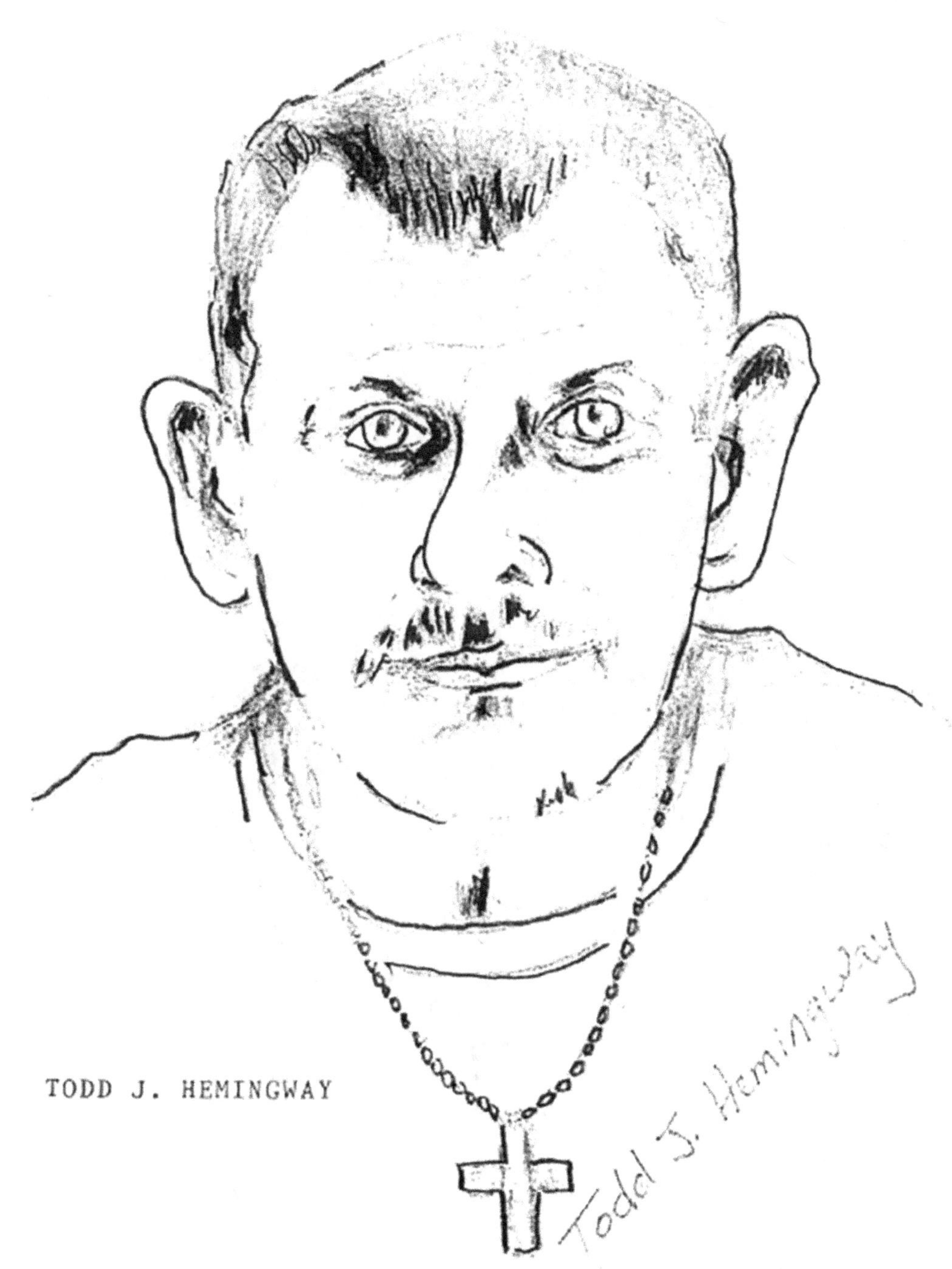

TODD J. HEMINGWAY

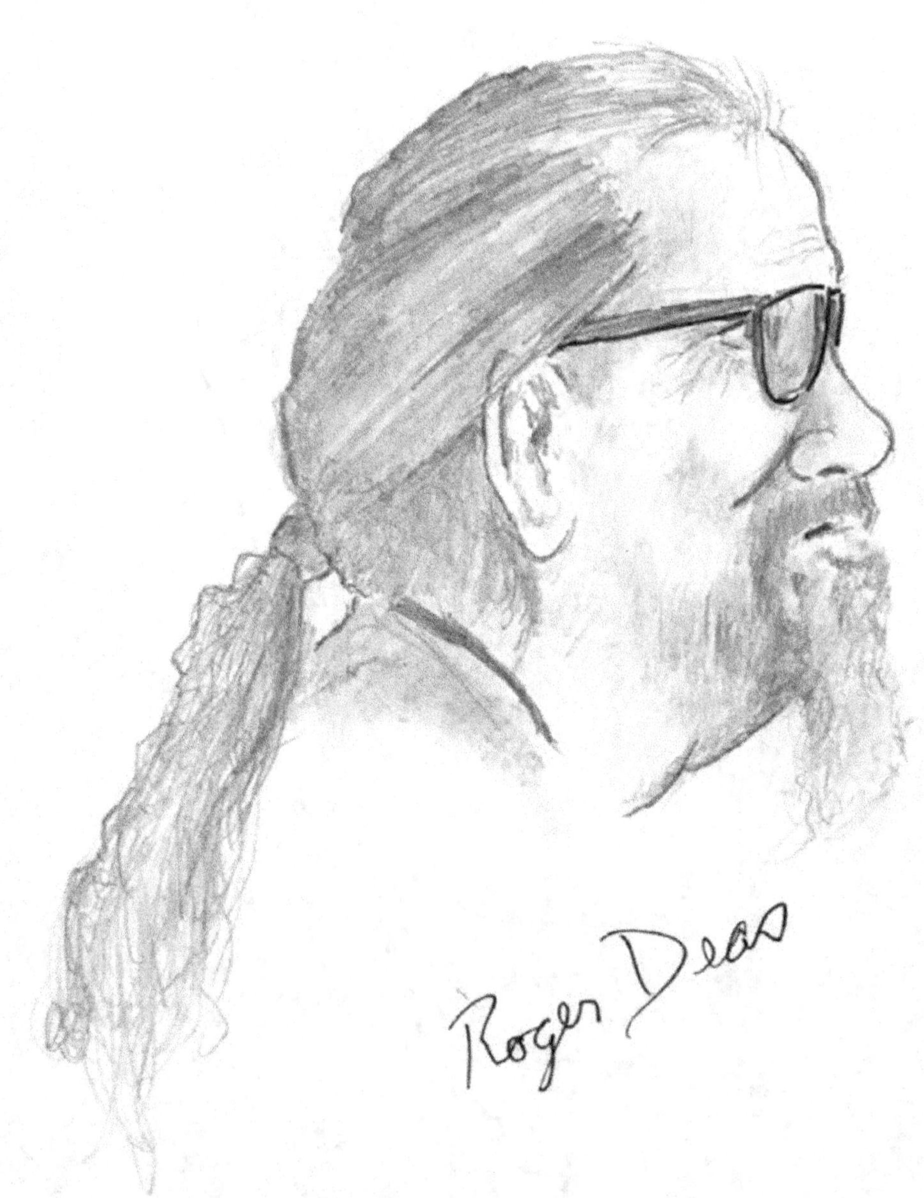

Roger Deas

WORDS

by Roger Deas

Where would we be without language?
How would we be able to connect?
And share ideas with other people?
How could we express our dreams and aspirations
Without reaching deep into our souls
And speaking our desires, fears, or longings?

Connection with others is a personal challenge
To be vulnerable to acceptance or rejection
To reveal who you truly are.
You can speak life and joy and healing,
Or you can crush a soul for life;
That is the power of the spoken word.

Consider carefully what comes from your lips.
Try to be positive in all you say
Because hurts will dig deep and fester,
Even turning the best of hearts
Into a bitter, cynical, outspoken rebel

Or a defeated recluse with no voice.

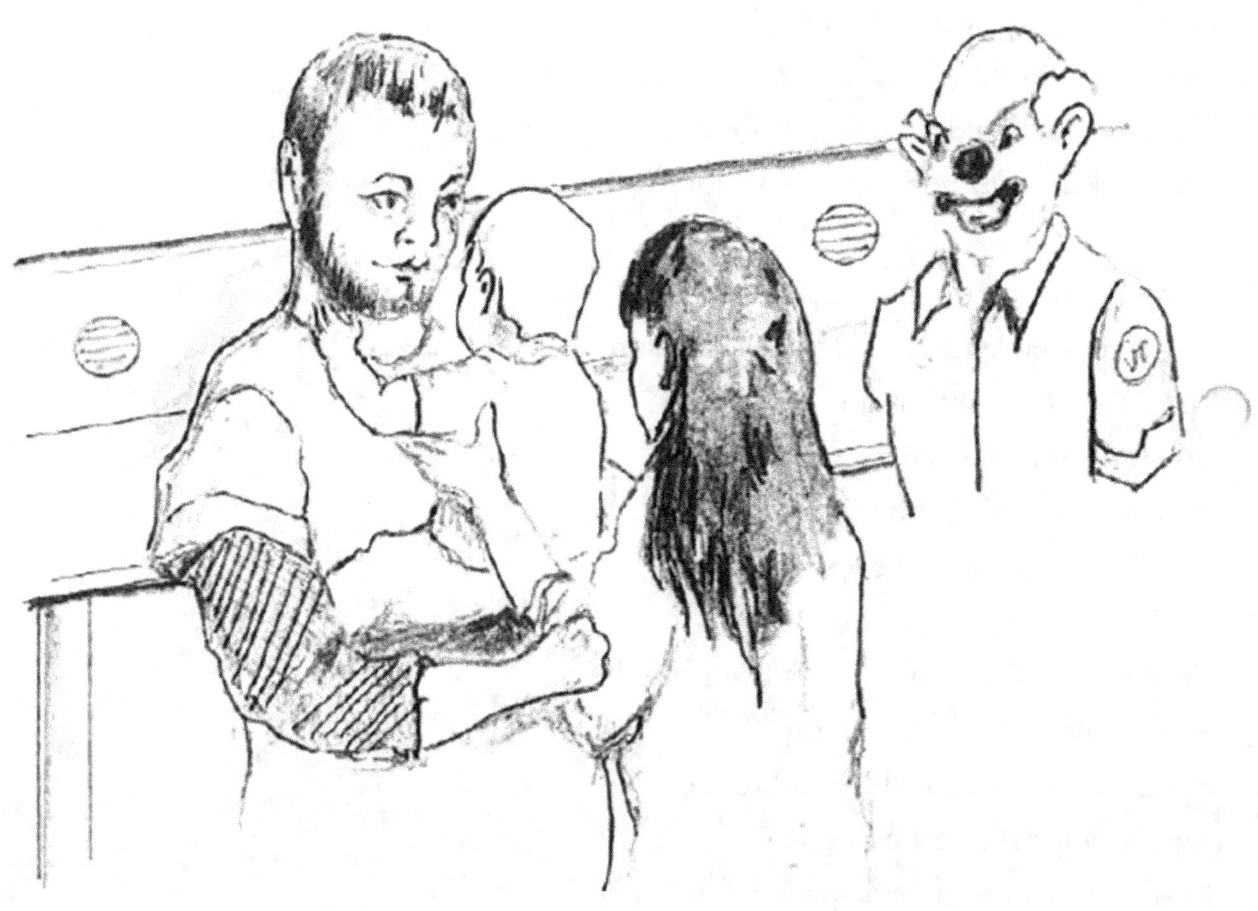

III. Silence

Some men drawn by Kolts chose not to contribute their writing. Out of respect for their decision, these men are still included in this section: Silence. We are left with Kolts' art as our mediator between us and the men, but without any text we are able to more intently engage with their physical expressions and gestures.

"Shaun Humphrey" stares ahead imploringly, his lips tight with consternation. He crosses his arms, revealing an identity bracelet that fetters his right wrist. The bracelet serves as a reminder of both the pervasive surveillance he and the other men are subjected to and the reduction of who they are to a trackable code.

Across from "Shaun Humphrey," Kolts depicts "Randall Gebo" with his eyes closed in resignation, seen through thickly framed glasses. His mustache imposes a frown on his otherwise muted expression. "16 ½ to Life | 2nd Degree Murder" is scribbled beneath him, providing jarring context for his imprisonment.

Hand gestures add dimensionality to the sketches of "Daren Arsenault" and "Darryl Beaumont." With his chin clasped in the purlicue of his hand, Daren Arsenault appears to be locked in contemplation, posing as if for a Greek sculptor. His sophisticated pose is balanced by his pedestrian crew cut hair. And like with "Shaun Humphrey," his identity bracelet cuffs his wrist, an inescapable indicator of his imprisonment.

The portrait of "Darryl Beaumont" has a more anxious quality to it. His hands are cupped around his mouth, either to rest his head in a sign of fatigue or to obstruct our view of his mouth as if to furtively conceal something. His eyes are cast down, and the corner of his mouth furrows with a shadow. With his overgrown sideburns and scruffy, unkempt hair, he looks hapless.

"P.S." exudes warmth and approachability. His face has a handsome symmetry that is conventionally pleasing. The roundness of his cheeks softens his appearance. His left eye and eyebrow are slightly raised, giving his countenance greater depth. His eyes are elegant and radiant, encompassed by long, intricately detailed eyelashes that are accentuated by the wrinkled lines beneath them.

The posture of "Robert LaBonte" is his portrait's most notable and unique feature. His large, slightly bulged eyes are lifted aspirationally, as if he is entranced by some higher hope or purpose. Thickly framed glasses and a protruding overbite present him with humble awkwardness. He looks kind.

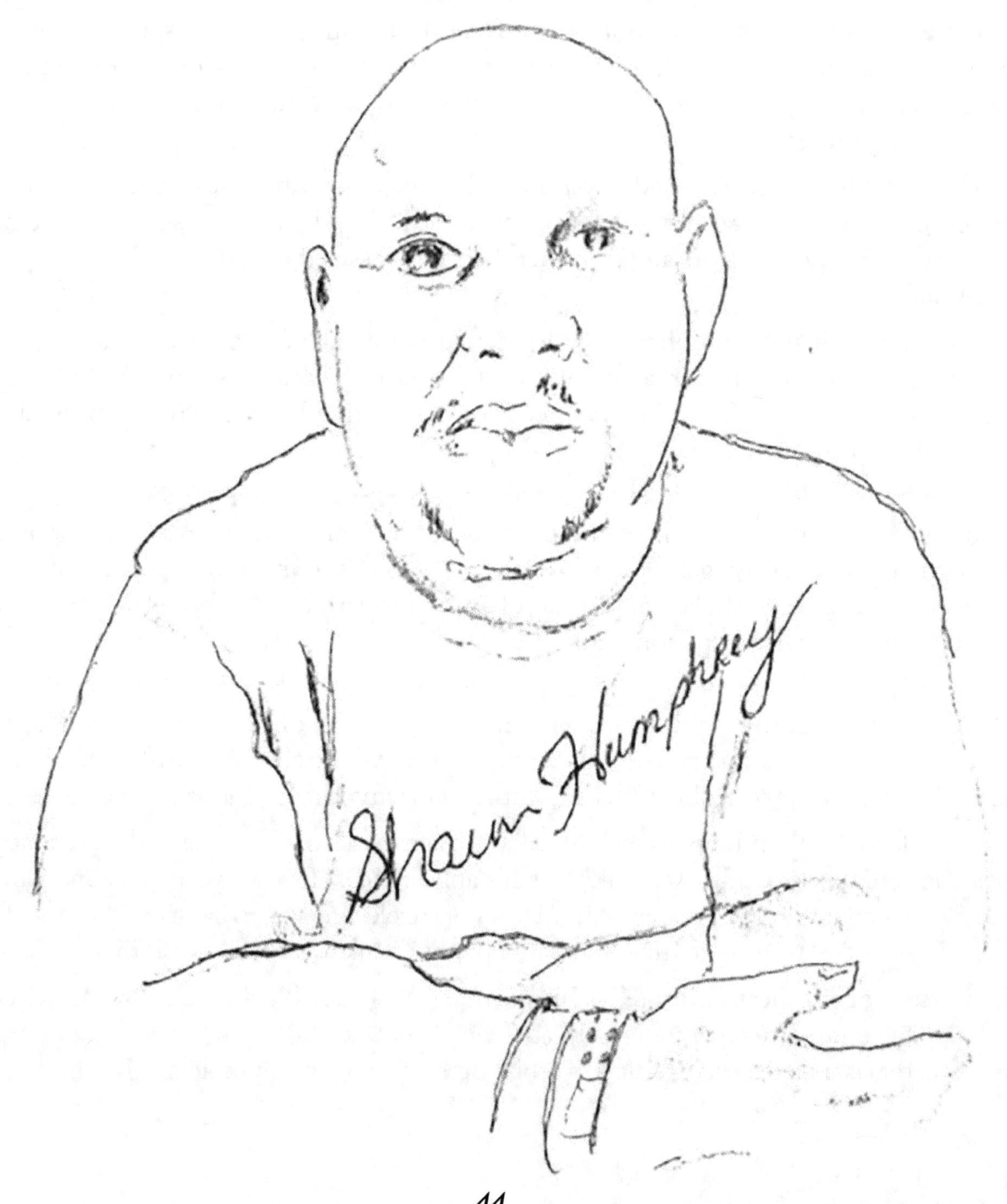
Shaun Humphrey

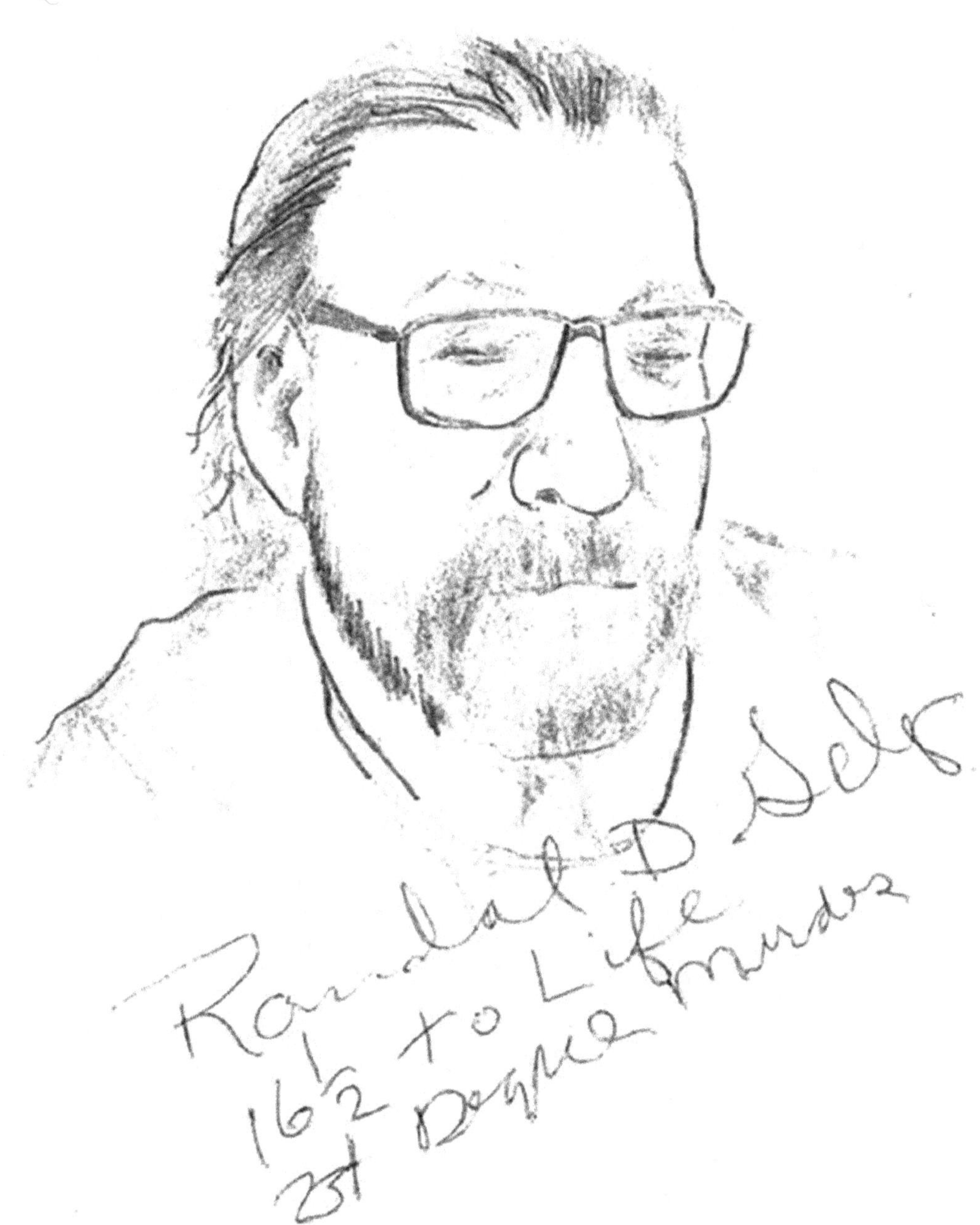

Randal D Sels
16½ to Life
2st Degree murder

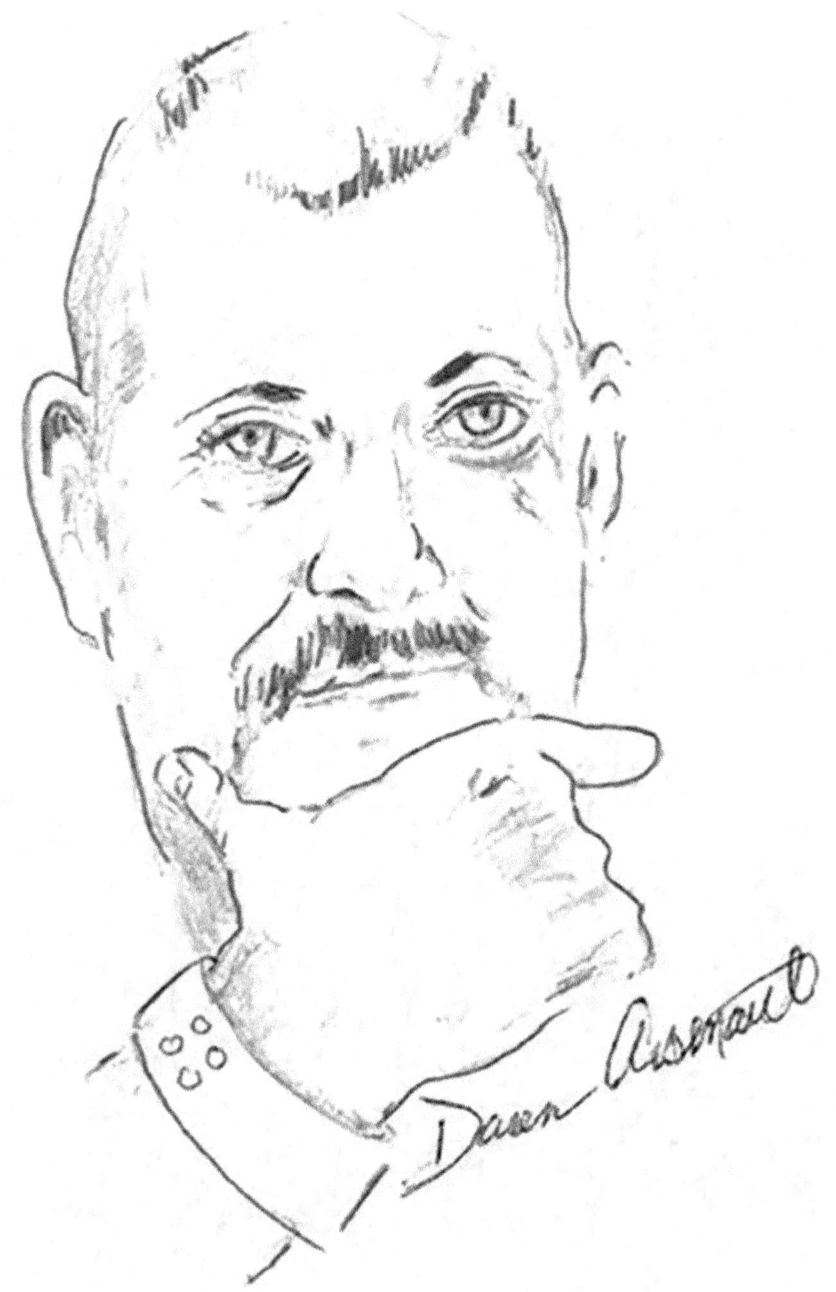

46

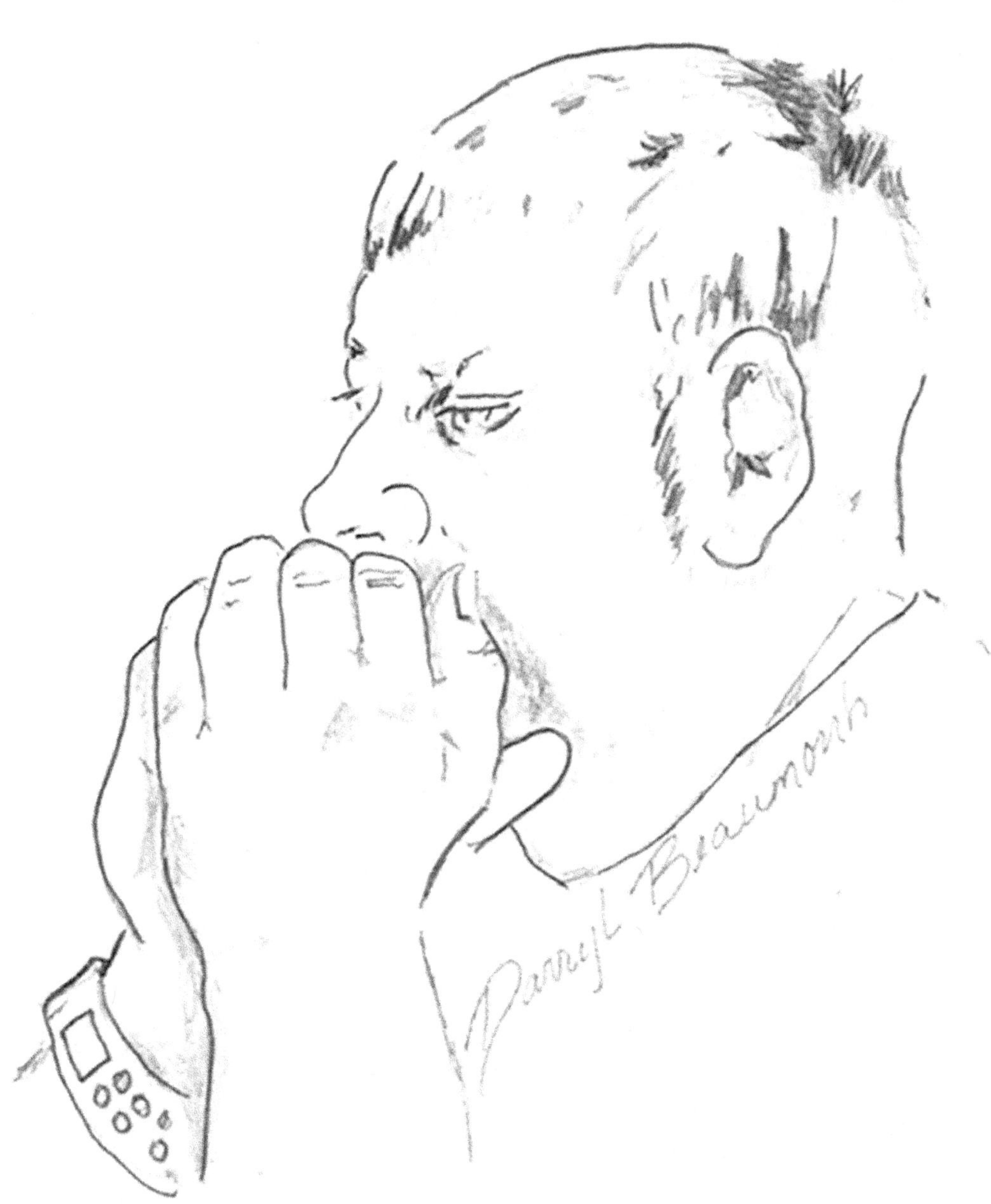

9/1/22 D.B.
NO CONTRACT
PIC ONLY
Darryl Beaumonth

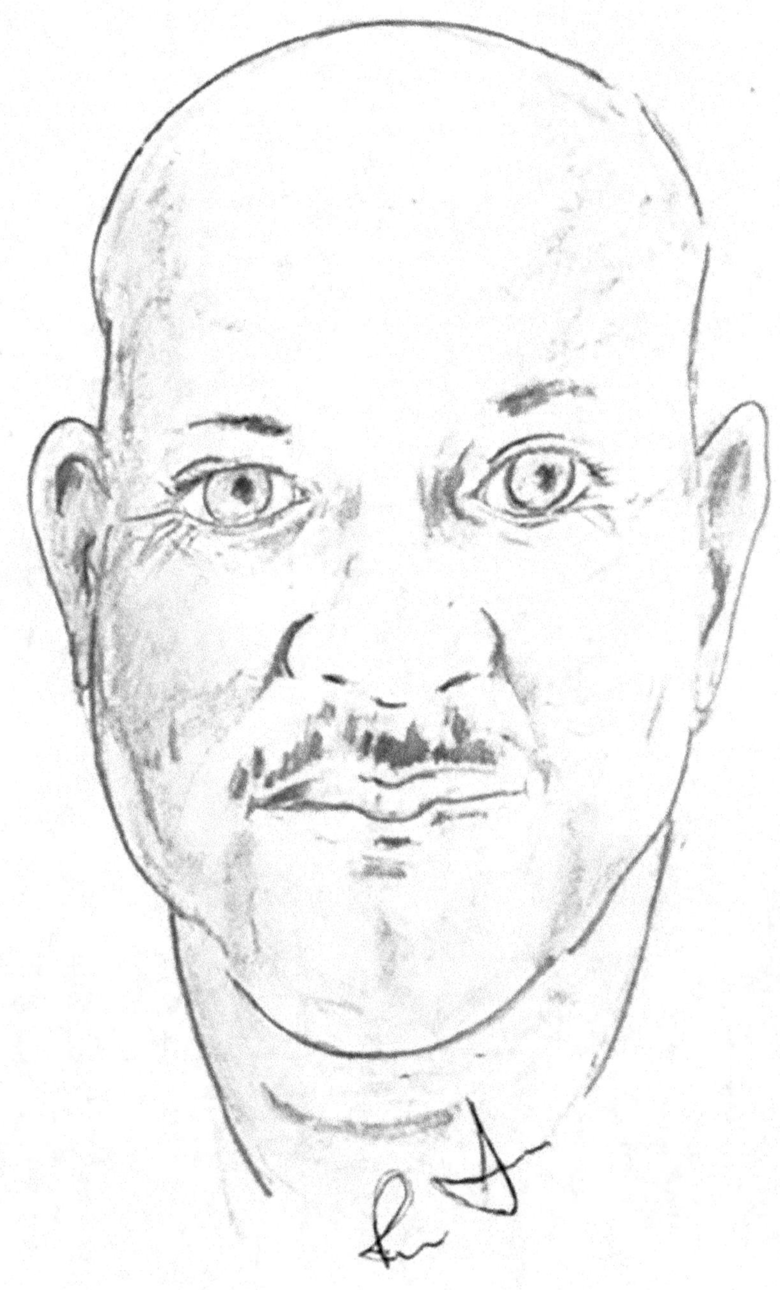

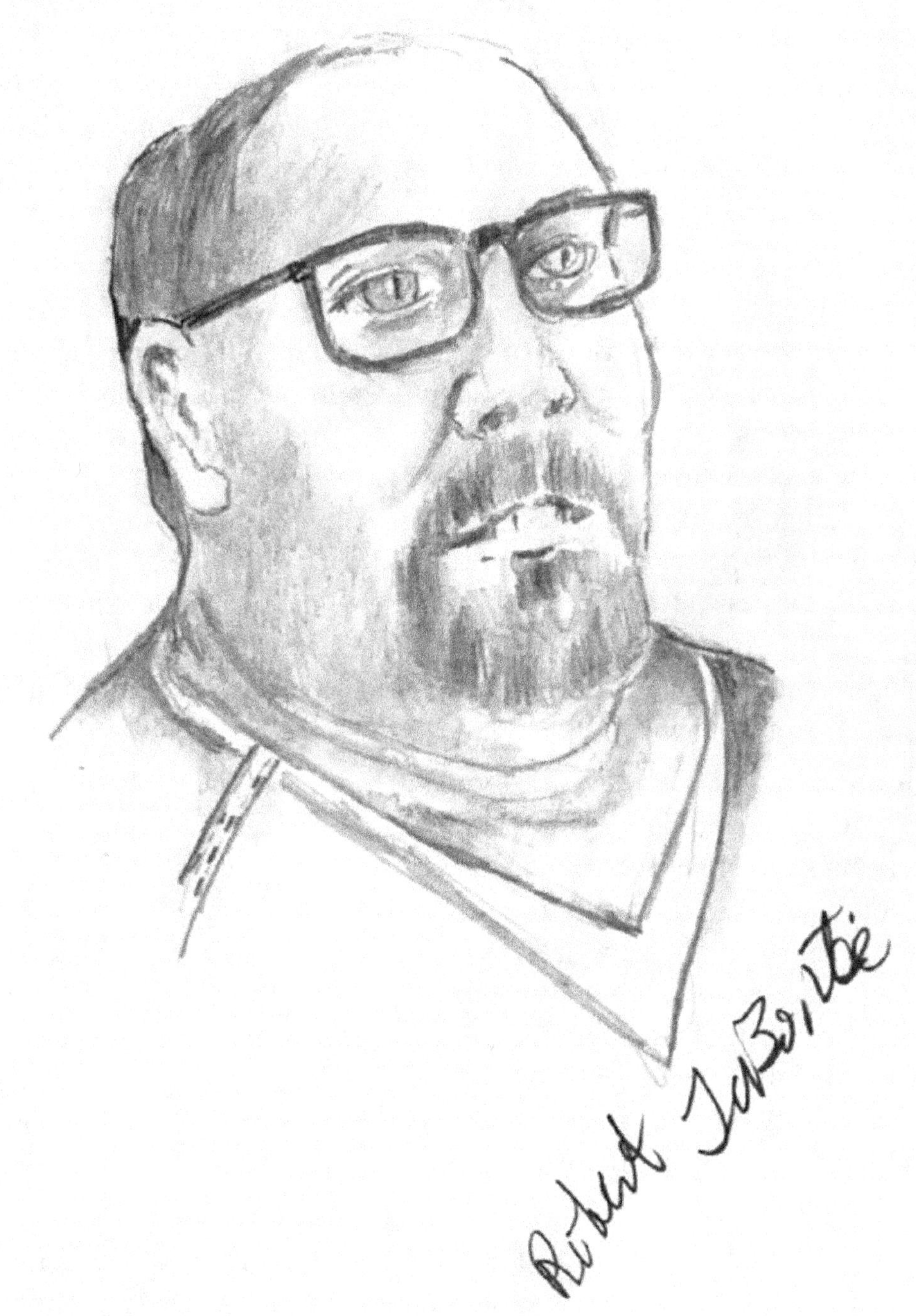
Robert LaBorde

IV. Faith

Prison is inextricable from morality. Crime and sin are, of course, closely related concepts. Prison and the words we associate with it—captivity, condemnation, judgment, punishment—often serve as corporeal metaphors that mediate our understanding of spiritual concepts like Hell, purgatory, or God's judgment. Likewise, spiritual concepts like redemption, grace, and mercy are deeply entangled with the intended purpose of various instruments of the criminal justice system, such as pardons and clemency. Within prison, however, faith is a fraught subject.

The first drawing included in Faith is a comical illustration of a classic feature of the criminal justice system: the religious cleric endeavoring to save the souls of the downtrodden sinner and criminal. In this case, a priest offers a rosary to a dumpster cat, symbolically extending an opportunity for the cat to repent for its sins and accept Christ. The priest smiles cartoonishly, flushed pink and cloaked in billowing robes. The cat, perched atop a garbage barrel, surrounded by empty bottles of liquor, and holding a half-empty pint of beer, responds to the priest's overtures literally: "My spirit, father? Just fine! Thanks for asking." The priest and cat's exchange, though amusingly unserious, captures well real dynamics between religion and crime—namely, the naivete of many aspects of prison ministry and the irreverence of many criminals. The portraits and writing that follows in Faith treat the subject of spirituality with considerable nuance and variation, reflecting the diversity of beliefs fostered by imprisonment.

Reflecting on the tragedies of his past, "William Kapusta" traces the deaths of his brother and mother to his spiritual awakening decades later. He emphasizes the power of prayer in his journey from desperately attempting suicide to faithfully accepting the weight of his sins and traumas. His faith in Christ empowers him to endure the horrors of prison, and to do so with compassion. His portrait reflects the spiritual maturity of his writing. Drawn in profile, "William Kapusta" appears dignified and sincere. He wears a trucker cap—an unassuming sartorial choice that evokes the relatability of the quotidian. The faint wrinkles on his neck and around his eyes express the strain and physical and emotional weathering he has endured. With his lips closed and stoical, his countenance almost seems reticent. His squinted eyes, however, allude to a sense of hope and contrition within him—a physical manifestation of the relief that accompanies his faith.

With the loquaciousness of a self-proclaimed ancient warrior-poet, "Jason Muxlow" expounds on a jeremiad of the hypocrisies of prison and the society that condemned him there. He seethes with virulence and righteous indignation as he denounces the impunity of prison officials and the dismissive condescension of the public. His verbiage is flamboyant but compelling in its harsh imagery: "some disabled con;" "ink-stained hump;" and "sheep in wolves clothing." He taunts us with vivid words that edge on vulgarity, imploring us to admit our discomfort in a disputatious exercise. His abrasive tone, however, is moderated by the sincerity of his aesthetic and intellectual curiosity. His "heart was stolen by the opera of Cyrano de Bergerac," he writes, showing off his unusually sophisticated taste. It is this aspect of his writing that is most compelling of all—he writes with total clarity and awareness of his audience and the class differential between the people who will read this book and the majority of the people contained within it. His prose stands alone in this regard. Though his style makes us uncomfortable in its uncanny awareness of our mores, tastes, and sensitivities, it is clear from his command of language that our discomfort is precisely his intention.

Kolts' sketch of "Jason Muxlow" is a moving accompaniment to Muxlow's writing. The vague contours of his tattoos on his arm and neck and the wheelchair beneath him visually amplify the imagery of his self-description. He is depicted in the act of writing, presumably that which is included alongside the portrait. He stares down at his work with focus and resolve, clasping his pen—the sword of the ancient warrior-poet. His writing may be inaudible, but his words are stentorian.

"George Smith" strikes a very different tone. Quiet humility is at the center of Smith's written prayer and the depiction of him in the act. He repeats "Father God" through his prayer, emphasizing his own subservience and God's paternal loyalty to His creation. Smith's hands are folded and raised to his head, his eyes and mouth are clenched shut, and he strains with intention—all physical signifiers of the exertion that thoughtful prayer requires. A book, likely the Bible, lays open in front of him. He concludes his prayer with meekness: "Your servant…"

The final texts of Faith consist of five poems that explore death and its unique associations for people in prison.

"Death—My Last Breath" traces death back to the moment of birth, and in doing so, it invokes the innocence of all of our beginnings. Our first breaths afford us no opportunity to transgress or do wrong. We simply are. Thereafter, we experience the formative trials that lead us to today. In the case of men in prison, those trials have included considerable misfortune. But in thinking of the arc of life, and our humble and pure first breaths, we remember that they too were once babies. And it was something else—something stronger—that imposed its evil on them.

"Death," a second poem by Roger Deas, whose portrait is included alongside his poem "Words" in Loss, is included in Faith. His words echo John Lennon in its imagination of spreading love and peace to the stars, but he offers a distinctly divine element, a "grander scheme." Death and what might follow it carries greater weight for those who are likely to die while incarcerated, as a future beyond death holds the only path to freedom.

The freedom that accompanies death is further attested to in the next poem "If I Die Tomorrow." The refrain, "Take joy cause now I'm free," is a common exhortation by the dying to those who will survive them, but it takes on new meaning in the context of prison. Freedom, here, carries not only the religious meaning of death liberating the spirit from the body to commune with its Creator, but for the prisoner, it is also literal freedom—release of the body from physical captivity, even if that body is no longer alive. The complexity of this concept is echoed by the portrait of the poem's author, K.C. He is depicted along with a book, with "If I die before..." sketched on its pages. He is fixated on the book, as if he were a monk or a sage trying to glean something prophetic from its text.

Edward Johnson's poem "Elegy of Death" is written with a whimsicality that contrasts starkly with its accompanying portrait. Witty rhymes about ugly tuxedos and bumping your head are juxtaposed with an unnerving sketch. The man, untitled, is oriented such that he would be making eye contact, except his eyes are closed. He clenches his eyes shut, purses his lips, and furrows his brow and forehead. He has a look of anguish, or of confrontation with death.

The final poem and portrait pair is that of "Kriss Valerio." His poem "Waiting" meditates on the anticipation of death. He has a balanced tone, with a hint of nostalgia, but more of an expression of acceptance. The portrait of "Kriss Valerio" carries similar solace and ease. He is shown in profile with his eyes closed gently, his mouth delicately agape, as if he is whispering. Round glasses, well-manicured hair, and a stylish beard with a ring give him a sagacious appearance.

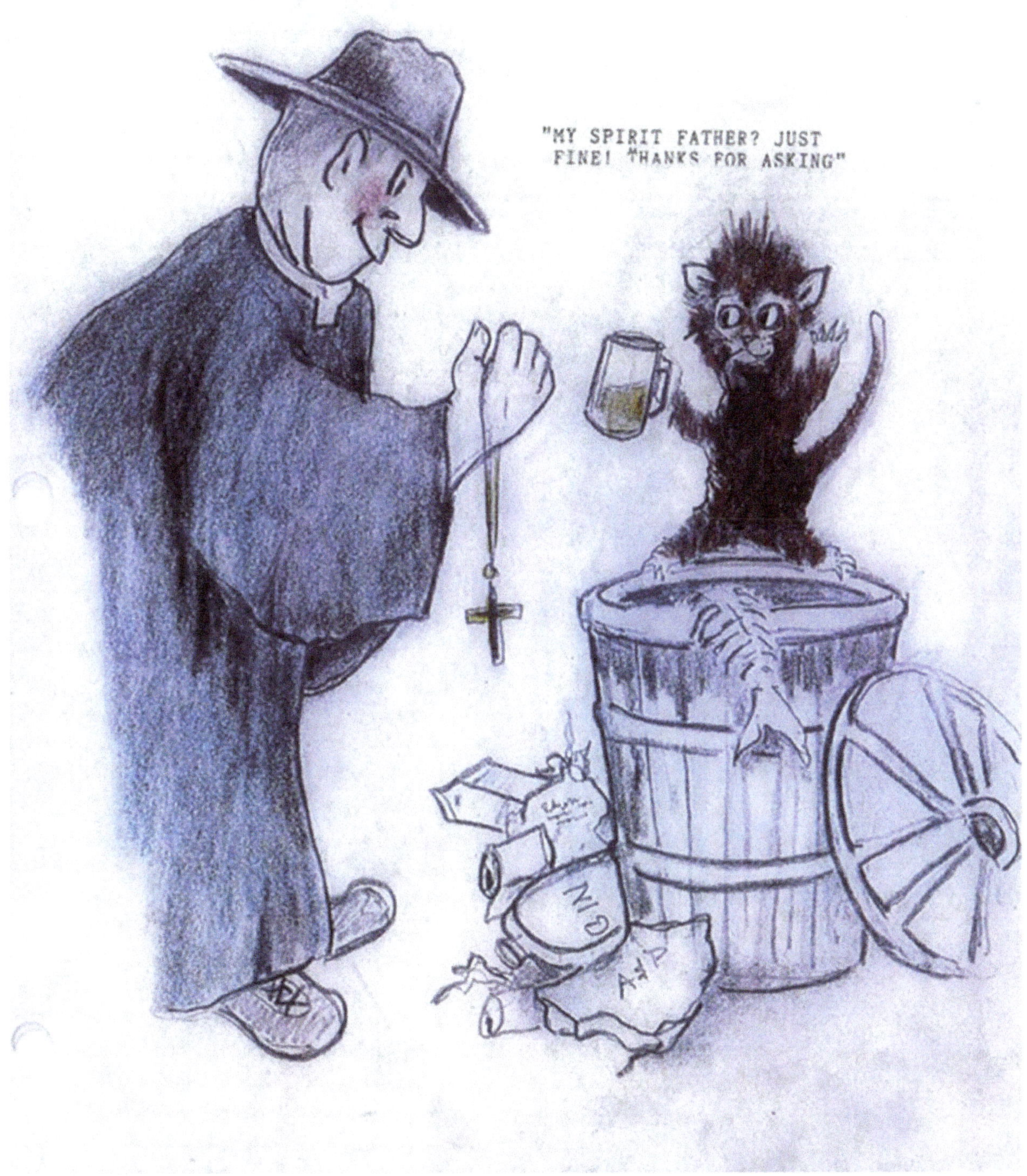

"MY SPIRIT FATHER? JUST
FINE! THANKS FOR ASKING"
GIN
A&P

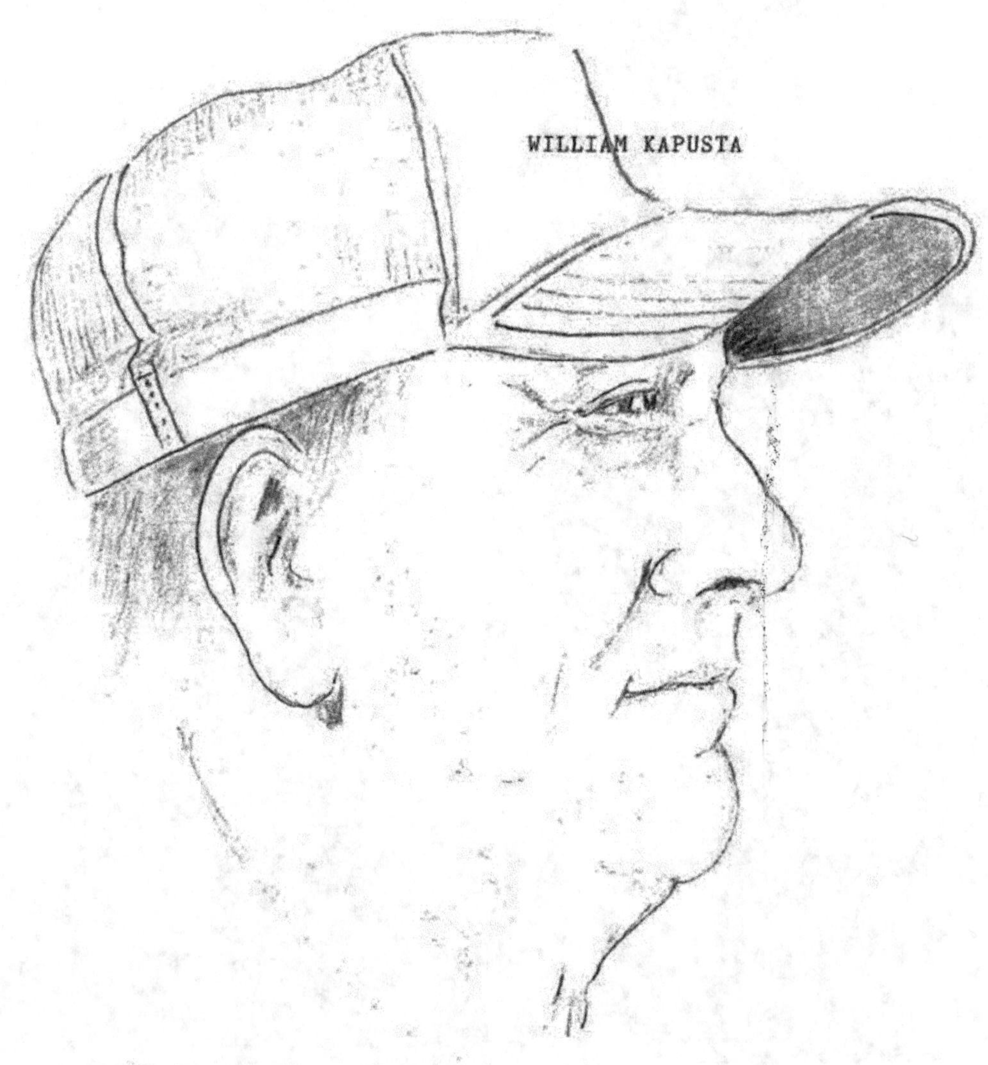

William Kapusta

William Kapusta

It was 1962 when we took a turn on a gravel road too fast and slammed into some old pines. My little brother and I were on our way back from a high school ball game. My friend had just gotten his license and picked us up in his parents' convertible. Past the rolled over car, I saw my brother laying in the middle of the road, covered in blood. A man knelt over him trying to breathe life back into him. I don't really remember if I actually saw that, but it was my last memory of the accident even to this day 60 years later. I don't even know if I was injured. I don't know how my family grieved or if there was a funeral. I don't remember how I acted when I went back to school or how I was treated — nothing.

In the spring of 1965, I returned home from basic training in Illinois. My mom worked evenings as a waitress, so I stopped in the house to see her before she left. I'd have to wait to see my Dad because he worked days at the marble quarry. She was so happy to see me. My older brother lived a few miles up the road so I walked over to see him not long after. As I was walking up the stairs to his apartment, his phone was ringing. Once he knew I was there he asked me to answer the phone because he was shaving. I said, "hello?" and my Mom was on the other end and said "Bill, I can't do this anymore."

The next thing I heard was two gunshots. The phone went dead. My brother and I rushed to her house and the last thing I remember was seeing my Mom laying on the floor, a revolver laying beside her. I don't remember my brother's reaction, any police talking to us, how my dad reacted, my brothers, or if I extended my leave or a funeral — nothing.

I've been in prison for 19 years. While it has been the greatest challenge of my life, going to prison has afforded me the time to reflect on my past and learn how I repressed memories to make life easier day to day. Eventually, I had to confront the pain I had experienced and the pain that I caused: I tried to take my own life. In the aftermath, I found new strength. I embraced my faith in Christ. Now, I never want to forget the pain, loss, and grief that I have felt and caused. I pray daily for those I've hurt so deeply. The power of prayer carries me through the horrors of my past and my present. The Lord helps me see my circumstances through his eternal eyes. I trust in Him. I shed my tears and they're no longer embarrassing because they are tears of compassion.

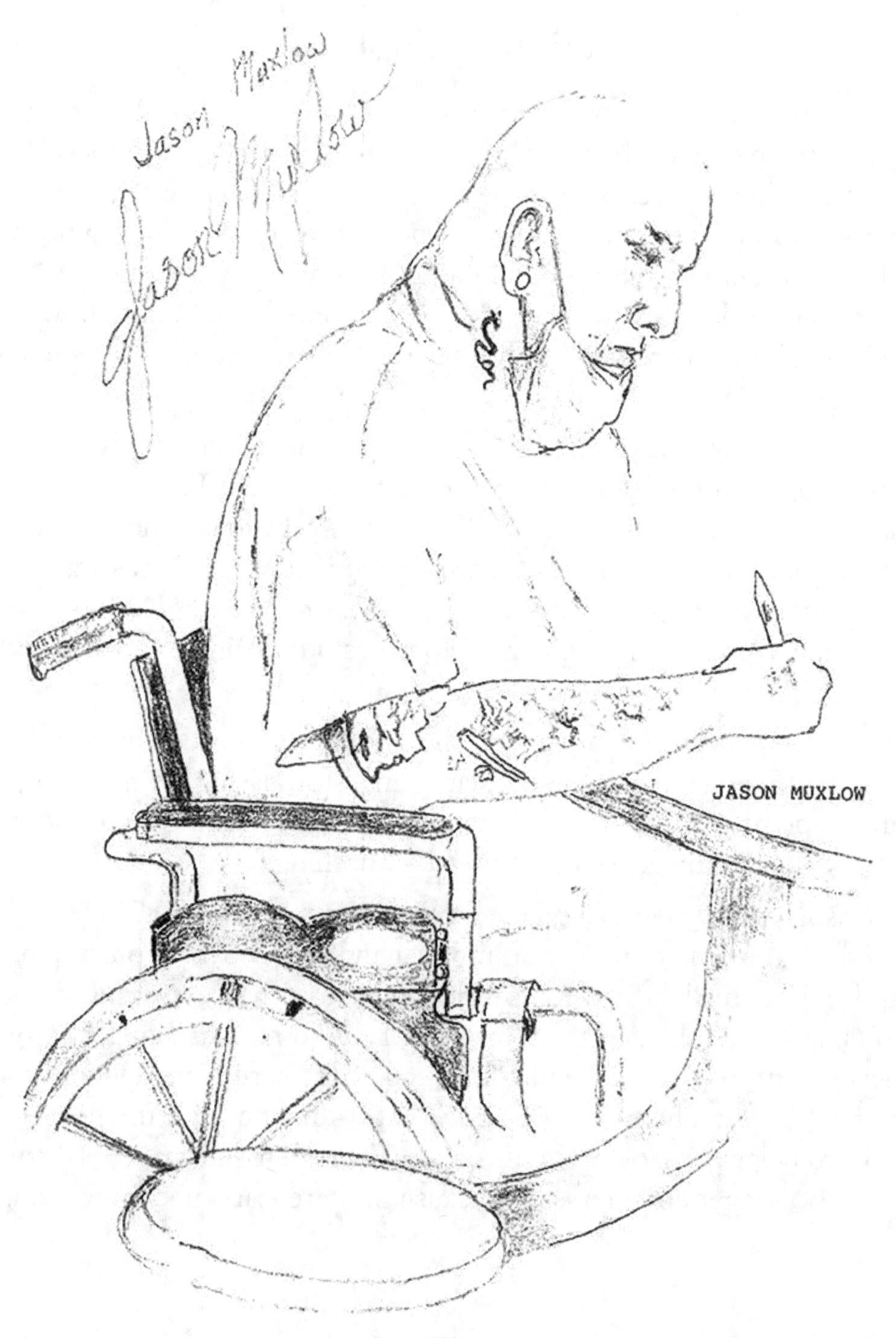

56

Jason Muxlow

Welcome to a sort of tragic and cruel living paradox, where the lofty and righteous who are tasked with the duty to carry out justice are themselves never held accountable for their misdoings. This is a place where naive passers-by may witness only some disabled con, skin littered with ink, and a scorned expression piloting a wheelchair, who's certainly earned such a penance resulting from a litany of unspeakable, immoral, vile conduct. The audience is unaware that he before them got that way because of the just and superior class. The ink-stained hump in the wheelchair once wished to be thought of as a polymath, and so doing led the life of an artist. A tattoo artist that loves poetry and had a heart of the ancient warrior-poet. He idolized men like Marcus Aurelius, Epictetus, Jesse James, Henry Thoreau, and Chip Foose. Whose heart was stolen by the opera of Cyrano de Bergerac. None will know this man has spent a large part of his life on two wheels. Two wheels that indeed once rode beneath him, instead of twain that now sit around him.

In fact, few may know that though others might consider him pious, he would never refer to himself as such. A clever and tactful exterior both conceals and unfortunately condemns the sheep in wolves clothing. A sheep who believes that fate is not preordained, but rather it is manufactured. Engineered by one's mind and produced by his deeds.

All men are capable of sin, and justice is served and upheld by men. In all of life, in nature there exist a system of order; spring must sprout and summer feed and grow before fall can wither and winter may snow. Men and justice must first produce fault before condemnation should cripple and slow!

George Smith

Father God, I pray for your blessings and your love. I am having a hard time and all I can think of is my family and God. Please forgive me for my sins, Father God. Please can you send my daughter my love and please shine your light over her and my family. I love you, Father God, and want to thank you for being with me, and please keep my family safe. Your servant...

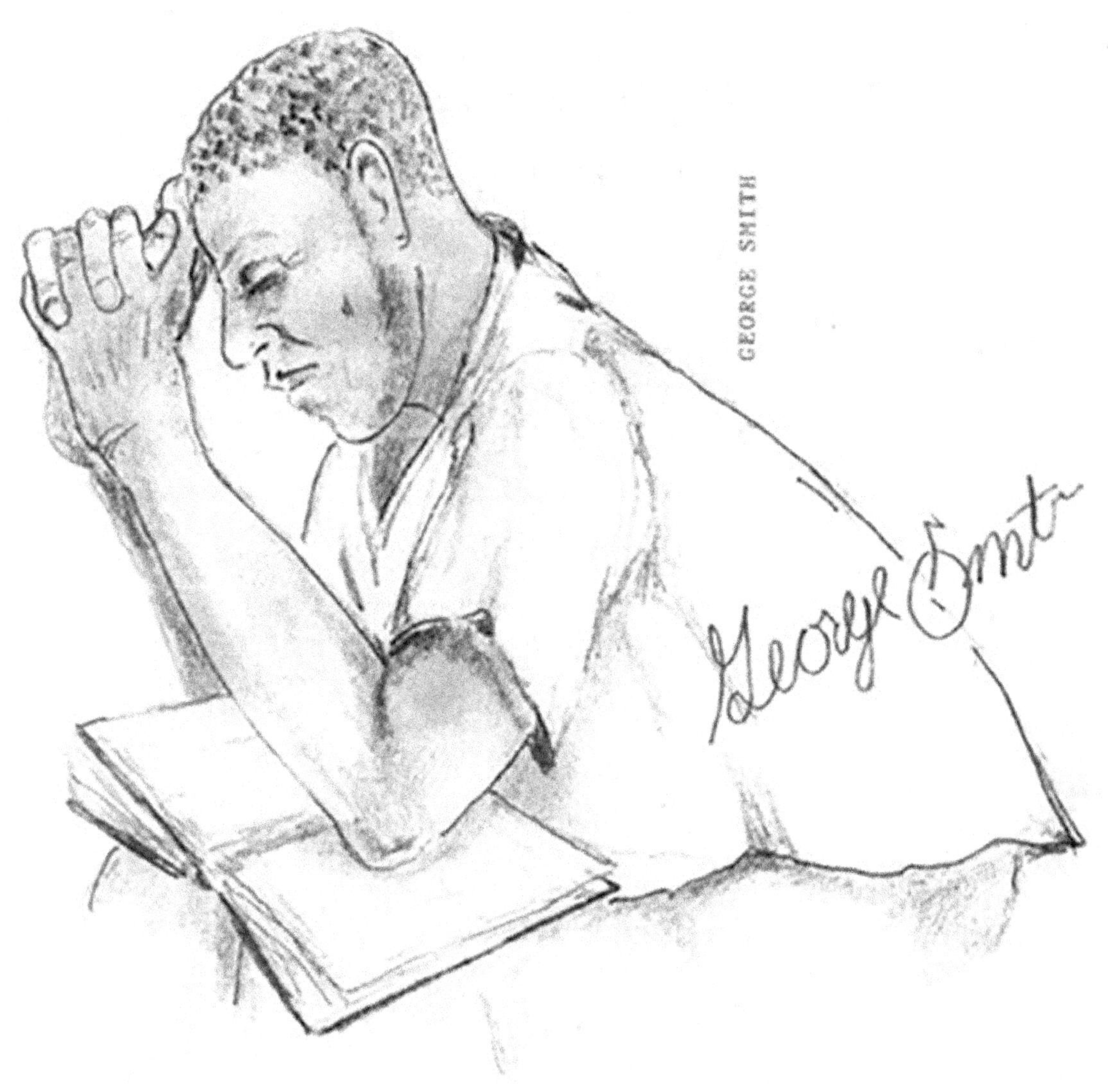

GEORGE SMITH

Death—My Last Breath

The first time I took a breath,
I knew nothing, felt nothing,
was nothing.
Not to myself.
I didn't know it took time to see,
to hear, to smell, to taste,
to touch, to think,
after all, it was my first time.
I didn't know it might take years,
many footsteps, many experiences
to find out how and where I was
going. I didn't know that I had
no choice in taking my first breath
    But finally, after all these
    years, I realize what my
    first breath was all about.
    It was about—
        MY LAST BREATH

DEATH
The first time I took a breath,
I knew nothing, felt nothing,
was NOTHING.
Not to myself.
I didn't know it took time too see,
to hear, to smell, to taste,
to TOUCH, to THINK,
after all it was my first time.
I didn't know it might take years,
many footsteps, many experiences
to find out how and where I was
going. I didn't know that I had
no choice in taking my first breath

    BUT FINALLY, after all these
    years, I realize what my
    first breath was all about.

    It was about—
       MY LAST BREATH

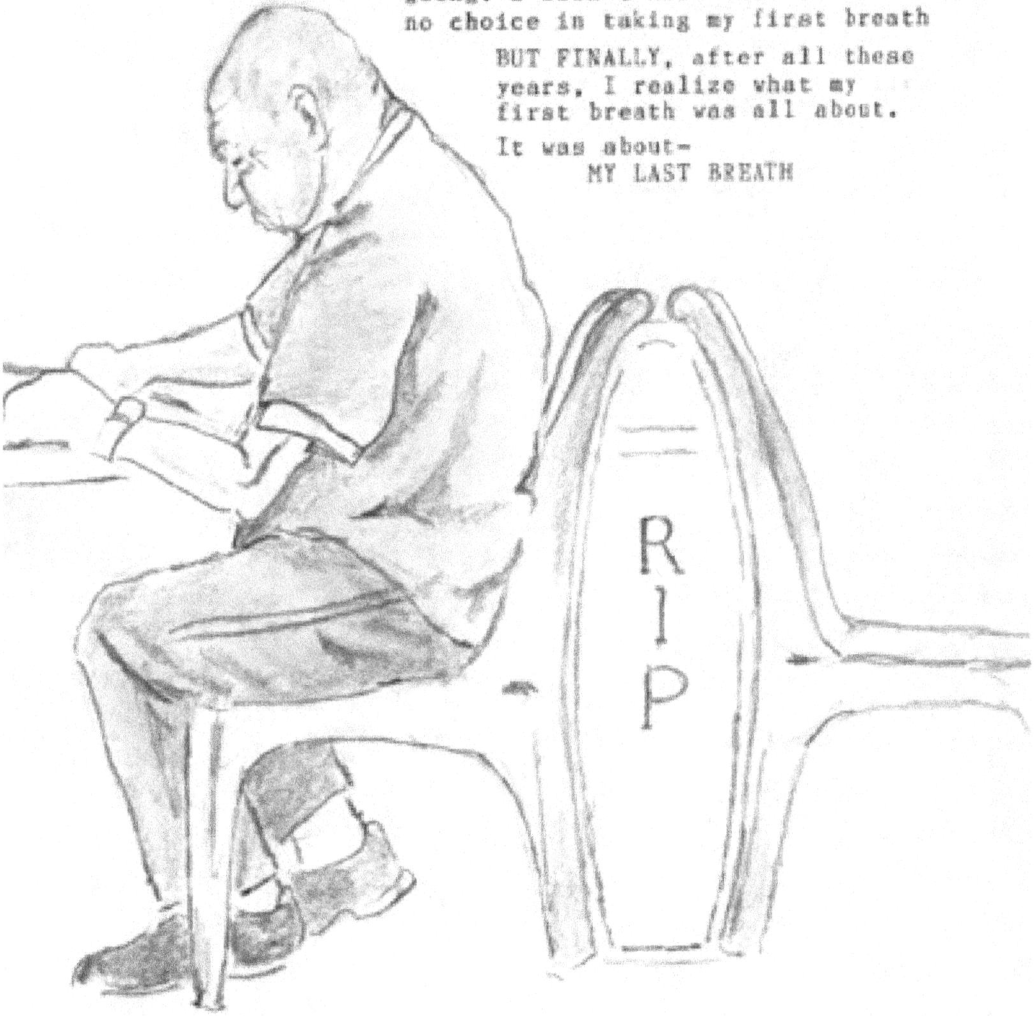

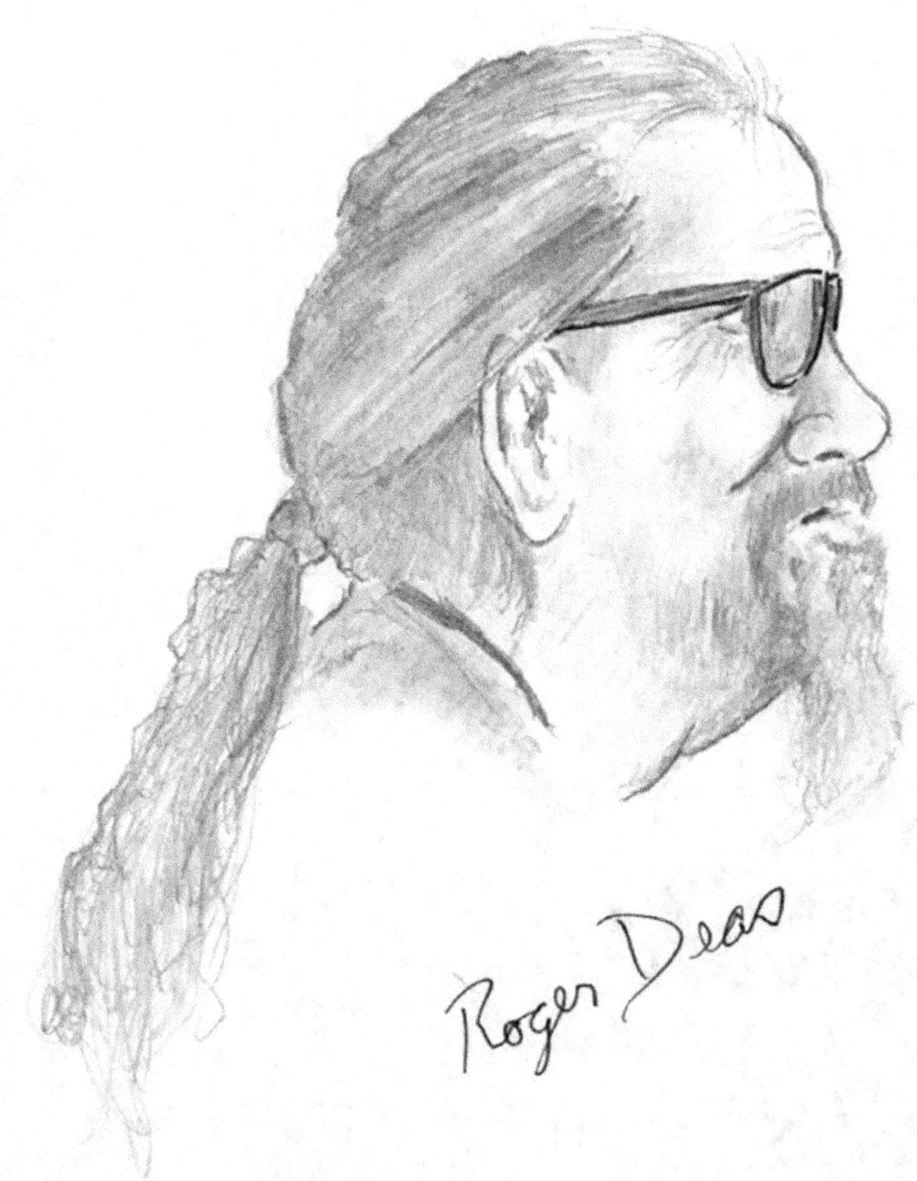

Roger Deas

Death

by Roger Deas

Death can arrive in many guises;
from illness, self-harm, accident, violence
or just the body naturally running down.

Many people fear it, some embrace it, and
some just accept the inevitable. Whether one
believes there is nothing afterwards, or
one is in paradise with 70 virgins, or
there is a true afterlife after a resurrection,
there is a transition in mind, body and spirit.

I believe that our Creator made a
way for an individual to be part of a
grander scheme: to teach and rule a
resurrected civilization that would not
only repopulate a renewed earth, but
would spread love and peace to the stars.

I can only imagine.

If I Die Before Tomorrow

If I Die Before Tomorrow
Please don't cry for me
Remember all our good times
Take joy cause now I'm free

If I die before tomorrow
Please don't shed a tear
instead shed off all your sorrow
Nothing good can come from fear

If I die before tomorrow
continue to be strong
Let go of all Resentment
Life will still go on

If I die before tomorrow
Please don't cry for me
Remember all our good times
Take joy cause now I'm free

K.C.

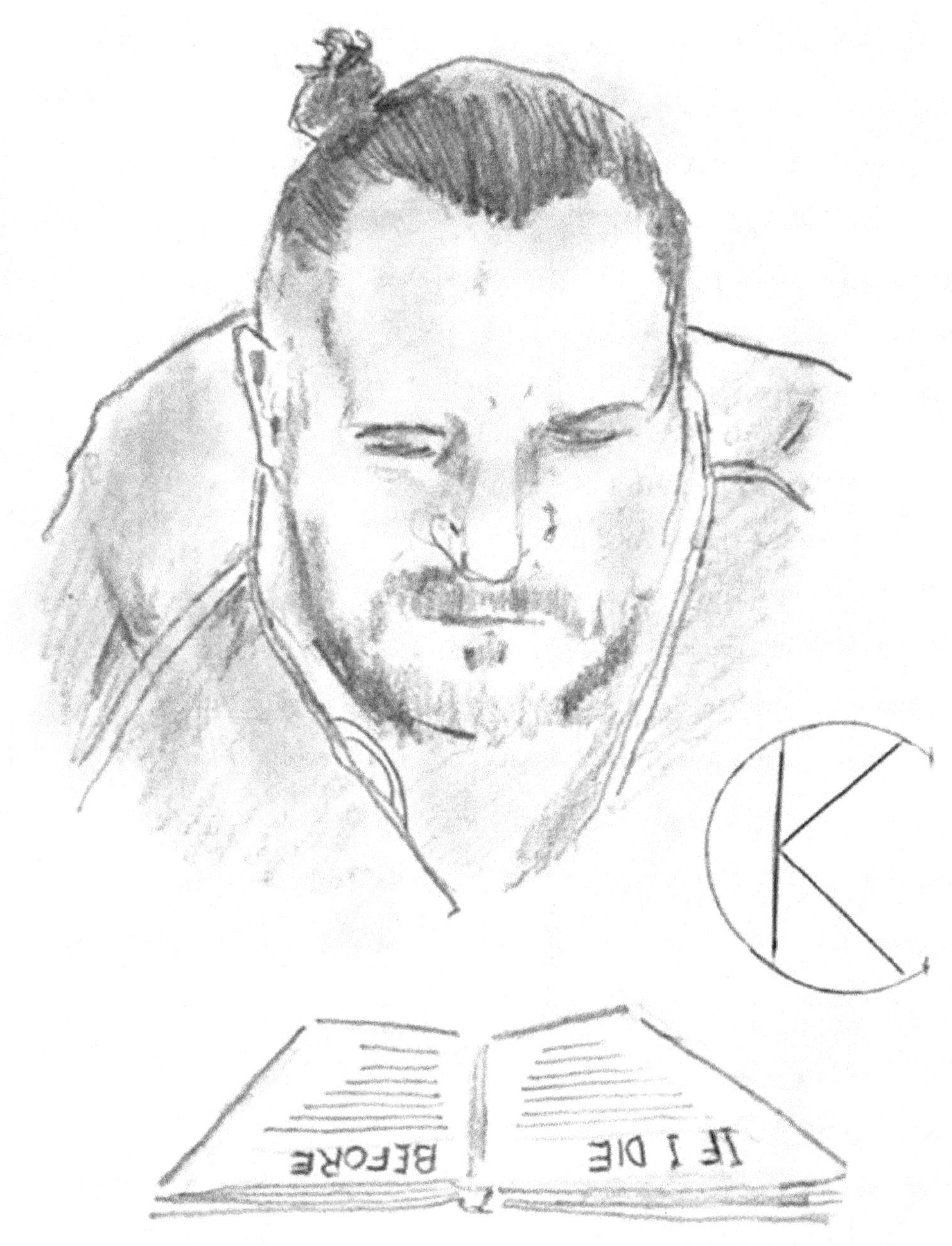

IF I DIE BEFORE

Elegy of Death

by Edward Johnson

You have a destination with your date
You don't know what to wear, you can hardly wait
It's a surprise, you take a deep breath
You have a feeling, a brush of death
You envy the living the most
You can't reach out cause you're a ghost
You come in this world with a nice suit
You're dead, your tux is ugly but you're still cute
"I could not stop for death,"
Emily Dickinson wrote about it and said it best
You hum along with the music clef
It's hard to remember the melody name left
You fell down and bumped your head
You see the savers but you're dead
You've lived a good life, your eulogy reads
Grim's here from Hell collecting his deeds
Your spirit roams from east to west
And your conscience travels through death.

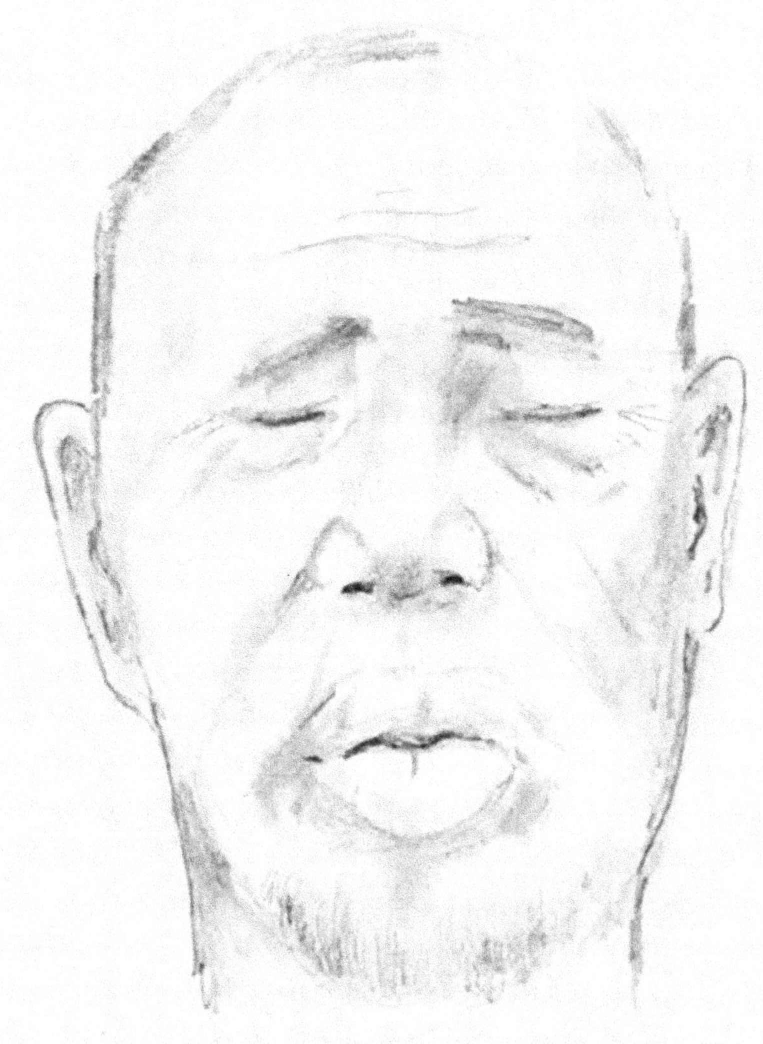

Waiting

by Kriss Valerio

Wish and wish, I can wish no more
It's time I open up that door
To do those things I long to do
Before the daisies push up through

Time rolls fast, looking upon the past
As we chisel, upon our stone,

      the loves of life are shown
      The passion, the heartache,
       the feeling we had
      I'll take all those times,
      The good with the bad.

      Will I see a familiar face,
      When it's time to leave this place?
      My family I miss,
      This I can't dismiss
      As I vanish into the stars,
      crowded in the sky,
      No longer, will I wait to die.

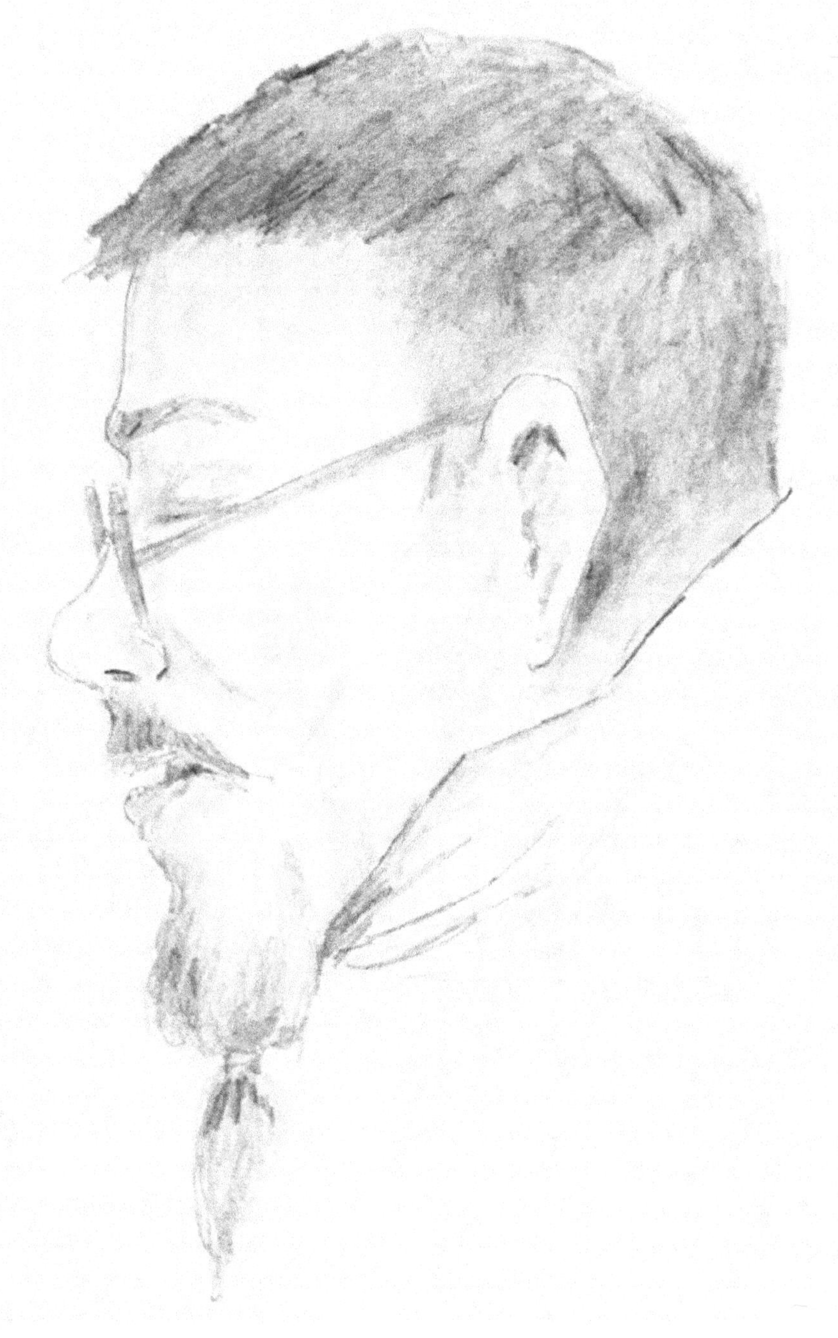

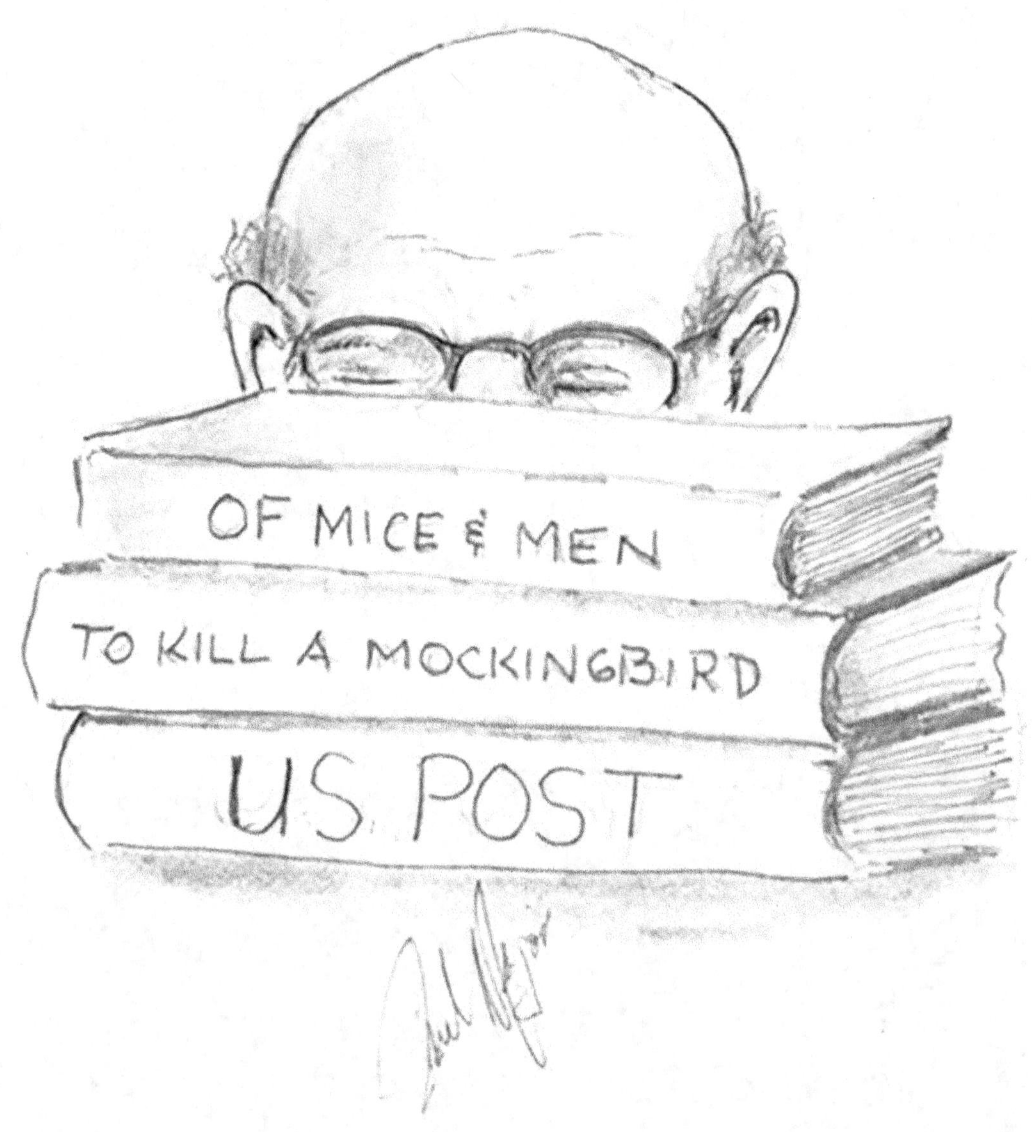

OF MICE & MEN
TO KILL A MOCKINGBIRD
U.S. POST

Afterword

The journey through this collection acquaints us with but an infinitesimal fraction of the people ensnared in American mass incarceration. The intimacy of Kolts' drawings and the literary voices of the included men aims to humanize a social problem that is more often than not expressed quantitatively. The numerical context of mass incarceration can be daunting in its scale. Art and literature, then, have the unique ability to empower us to action in ways that data and research do not. Data do not fail to move us because of their inaccuracy or insufficiency, but rather because of the debilitating horror of their inerrancy. Culture holds incredible power to translate aspects of society that can seem opaque or disconcerting into forms we can understand and sympathize with, culminating in a desire to improve the conditions we see to be deficient.

For no one in respect to prisons was the power of cultural cache more potent than the aforementioned Johnny Cash. Long before Johnny Cash wrote his prison anthems, Cash himself was moved by another artistic work: Crane Wilbur's 1951 film Inside the Walls of Folsom Prison, which later served as the basis for his song "Folsom Prison Blues." Inside the Walls of Folsom Prison implores viewers to see the error of using incarceration strictly as punishment and to embrace the potential for rehabilitation. While the film pursued this message rather bluntly, Cash saw how he could use music to deliver a similar, but subtle message—namely, through humanizing the criminal, the outlaw, and the prisoner. He created massively popular and relatable artistic expressions of the plight of prisoners that resonated with a mid-century public otherwise mired in the Civil Rights Era and skeptical of reform. Cash's criminal was an American—a figure of Americana that we could root for against our baser instincts. So moved by his humanization of the people imprisoned in our country, the United States Senate even requested that Cash testify before the Judiciary Committee on the topic of prison reform. The power of art reverberated into national politics.

The aim of this collection is to catalyze more conversation, more art, and more action in regards to prisons and the people locked away in them. Humanizing people on the margins of society, especially those whom some consider evil or corrupt, is no easy task. But making room for the faces and voices of incarcerated people, and amplifying them when they present themselves, are good places to start.

About the Artist

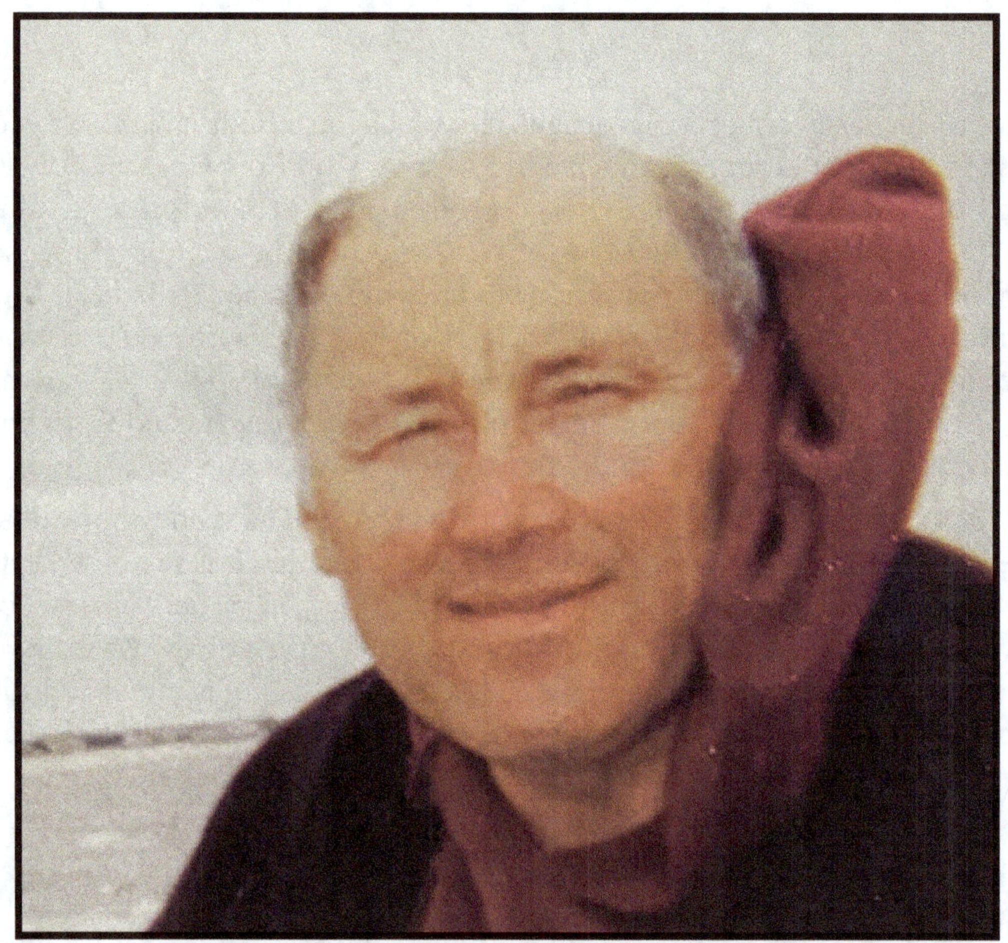

Rein Kolts was born on March 1, 1946, in Seeboden Austria. In the aftermath of World War II, Rein and his family of seven became sponsored refugees in North Carolina. While in college in the 1970s, he became interested in art through his visits to the exhibitions at the Rhode Island School of Design. Rein's career focused on civil engineering, but after his retirement he immersed himself in his favorite mediums—oil and watercolor. He was a prolific artist prior to his incarceration in 2014. His decade of incarceration has been consumed by his appeals and litigation, which have found favor at the Vermont Supreme Court and U.S. Court of Appeals for the Second Circuit. Rein continues producing art while incarcerated, primarily portraits of his fellow inmates.

About the Author

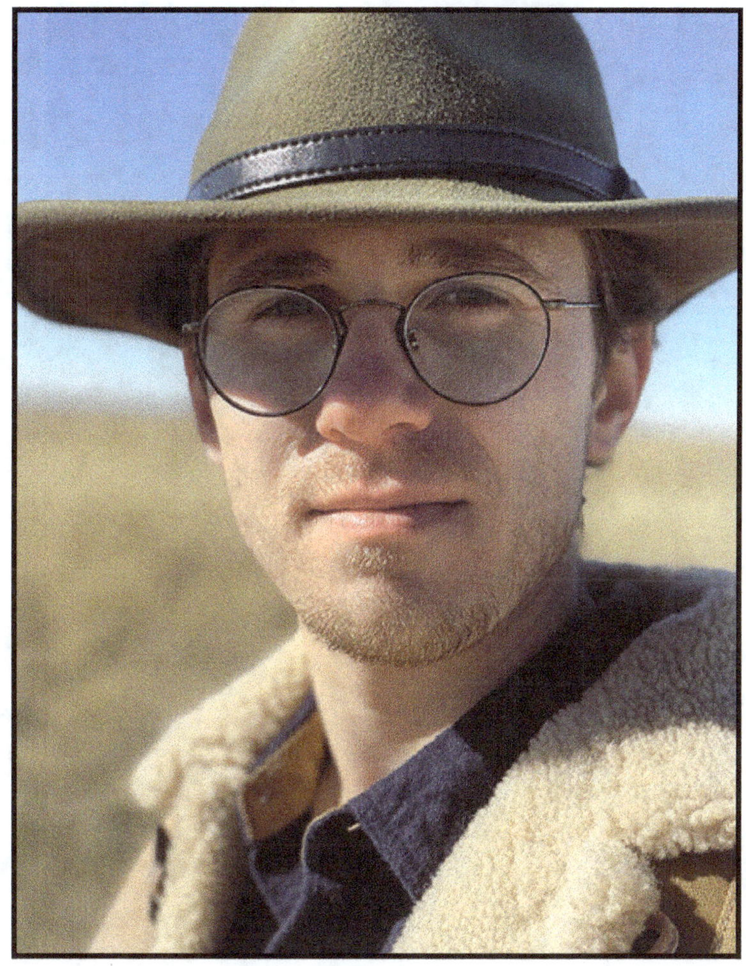

Devon Kurtz was born in Westfield, Massachusetts. He graduated Phi Beta Kappa with a Bachelor of Arts in Classics from Dartmouth College, where he first became interested in the intersection of faith and prisons. Devon studied correctional chaplaincy at Wheaton College while starting a Quaker ministry at Southern State Correctional Facility in Springfield, Vermont. His work follows in a long tradition of prison ministry among Quakers at Hanover Friends Meeting, of which Devon is a member. He is currently a graduate student in criminology and penology at Homerton College, University of Cambridge. He splits his time between Vermont, Utah, and England, accompanied by his Australian Cattle Dog, Odetta.